ECHO IN CELEBRATION:

A Call To Home-Centered Education

SECOND EDITION

LEIGH BORTINS

CLASSICAL CONVERSATIONS MULTI-MEDIA

D1052458

Echo in Celebration
A Call to Home-Centered Education

Second Printing, 2008
First Printing, 2007
Printed in the United States of America

ISBN 0-9798333-0-2

Dedicated to my husband, Robert, who thought it was a good book.

Echo In Celebration

Contents

Acknowledgements

I would never have written this book if my boys hadn't asked me the same questions over and over, proving to me that classical education is God's method of instruction.

I could never have written this book without repeatedly watching Andrew Pudewa's "Student Writing Intensive" videos.

If this book is of any value, it is because thousands of parents have asked me the same questions over and over again. You challenge me to think clearly and articulately. I'm not sure if I actually do think clearly and articulately, but you make me try. The learning comes from the trying.

Thank you to my family for giving me up each summer as I speak and write.

Thank you to Heather for doing anything it takes to get the words out of my brain and onto paper.

Thank you to Leah, Denise, Jennifer, Erin, Kathi, Cyndi, Keith, and Janet for editing and layout.

Thanks be to God that His mercies are new every morning.

Chapter One

The Passion: Loving Life and Learning

"It is not the critic who counts; not the man who points out how the strong man stumbles, or where the doer of deeds could have done them better. The credit belongs to the man in the arena, whose face is marred by dust and sweat and blood; who strives valiantly… who knows the great enthusiasms, the great devotions; who spends himself in a worthy cause; who at best knows in the end the triumph of high achievement, and who at the worst if he fails, at least fails while daring greatly, so that his place shall never be with those cold timid souls who have… known neither victory nor defeat."
—Theodore Roosevelt, Sorbonne lecture, 1910

O ne of my favorite books is *Exuberance: The Passion for Life*, by Kay Redfield Jamison. The first chapter, read in a restaurant, inspired me to walk a mile in 35-degree weather past a windy New England waterfront, rather than take a taxi, just so I could feel more of life. I was very cold, but I spent 30 minutes reveling in a fisherman in a bright yellow dory, the song of automobile wheels on a 100-year-old bridge, a set of armor on a porch, lace curtains in a Colonial window, and lots of "hellos" to bundled up strangers.

I live and breathe life and learning. Jamison's book made me want to share, with anyone who would listen, the joy and enthusiasm that results from living a life grounded in the exuberant love of learning — or rather, playing hide and seek with God as He reveals His creation (Prov. 25:2). Life may often be very hard, but it should never be really boring.

Consider Jamison's words:

> "...it is the infectious energies of exuberance that proclaim and disperse much of what is marvelous in life. Exuberance carries us places we would not otherwise go — across the savannah, to the moon, into the imagination — and if we ourselves are not so exuberant we will, caught up in the contagious joy of those who are, be collectively inclined to go yonder. By its pleasures, exuberance lures us from our common places and quieter moods; and — after the victory, the harvest, the discovery of a new idea or an unfamiliar place — it gives ascendant reason to venture forth all over again. Delight is its own reward, adventure its own pleasure" (p.4) [1].

As I study the words of Francis Bacon, Teddy Roosevelt, Augustine, and others that loved, tackled, and savored life; it makes me want to encourage others to inspire that same hunger in our youngest citizens — our children. I have been led, no — impelled, to teach my four children with our home as their 'base camp' since 1983, and I plan to continue until our youngest, David, is launched in 2015. My husband I plan to home school 32 years.

I take seriously the injunction of Jesus that if I cause my children harm I may as well hang a millstone around my neck and jump in a lake (Mark 9:42). For His sake, I'm driven to inspire my children with a love of life and learning that overflows from their spirits even in the most difficult of situations. I'm compelled to "ride horses up the White House stairs" as Teddy Roosevelt did with his children, and I want to share with them the deep sorrow rather than self-righteousness that comes from the ugliness of sin. I want them to work so hard and to have fun so physical each day that they can't wait to climb into bed each night. I want them to know that everyone they encounter can be their teacher, and that they are to inspire each person they meet to draw a little closer to our Father in heaven. Life is but a vapor, and yet it's also a divine journey — a journey that can result in unspeakable joy and heart-satisfying peace that passes all understanding.

Our Family's Journey

Our journey as a family began in 1983 when my husband, Rob, and I were married while we were students at the University of Michigan studying aerospace engineering. He is very quiet. I was introduced to him as "Bob" Bortins and proceeded to call him that until our wedding day. My mom and my aunts arranged for all the pertinent wedding apparatus to be engraved with "Bob and Leigh." Toward the end of our wedding reception, Rob just leaned in to my ear and whispered, "My name is Rob. I don't like Bob." I still chuckle whenever I see the wedding knife in the kitchen drawer. And I am still trying to get to know this quiet, humble man.

When I graduated from Michigan, I found myself with a husband and baby Robert and some hard choices to make. When I was a new mom, I wanted everything to be just right for my baby and I, which I know now is a definite contradiction! I wanted to work at the career I had studied so hard to prepare for, and I wanted to be home full-time with Robert. Well, selfishness won, and I went to work at Boeing Military Airplane Company. Then a funny thing happened — I saw a talk show called "Donahue" (revealing my age) where they interviewed a strange looking family concerning their choice to home school their children. I thought the family was incredibly peculiar, yet they inspired me to want to home school. In my confused mind, I was going to home school while I worked full-time. Amazing how inconsistent I can be! Anyway, for the first time in my life, I was a lousy employee because all I could think about was Robert at home without me.

I became pregnant with John and quit working the very day my Boeing contract ended. I worried about what my parents would think. After all, they were the ones that said, "Don't be the nurse, be the doctor. Don't be the secretary, be the CEO. Don't be the stewardess, be the pilot." And they were the ones who had been proactively directing my education all along. When I called to tell them the changes, they surprised me by being very proud of my decision to be a full-time mother. They had worried about Robert being raised by someone else. My mom said, "I stayed home with you guys when you were little, and I have a great career now. Work can wait. Robert can't." And so, for me, the hard work of guiding a young child to passionately love life and learning began.

Rob and I have raised four sons together in a variety of states and homes. All of our boys have had their education centered in our home so we could share with them our love of life and learning. Our eldest son has graduated from college with an engineering degree, and our second son is studying at a Appalachian State University for a bachelor's degree in construction management. We had a 10-year gap where several pregnancies weren't carried to term until we were finally blessed with two more healthy boys whom we continue to teach and encourage from our home.

Currently, Rob and I both work from our home, though we have had a myriad of job situations over the years in order to keep us fed and still have someone home to teach our boys to love life. We have both worked full-time away from home, full-time in the home, and part-time out of the home. Has it been easy? No, but we know we are accountable should our boys become part of the 40 percent of U.S. high school students who graduate each year unable to read simple books like *The Hardy Boys* series. We are accountable should they become part of the 40 percent of all Americans who don't even graduate from high school (See appendix.).

We want our children to spend the bulk of their formative years observing responsible behavior modeled by adults and children who like to serve God with their families.

Home-Centered, not Home-Shackled

Though our schooling has been home-centered, we definitely haven't spent much time at home. We were blessed to have my husband work for an airline when it was still easy for employees to travel for free. So Robert and John, my older two boys, have camped in the Olympic Rain Forest, climbed Mt. St. Helens and Mt. Rainier, stood in the Mississippi River, and swum in almost every major body of water in and along the United States. They've been to a number of foreign countries on mission trips and have had lots of fun visiting friends and relatives. Travel would have been limited if they had had to follow someone else's academic calendar.

William and David, our younger two, haven't had the benefit of free airfare, yet we've still managed to hike in the Rockies a few times and travel up and down the East Coast. One winter, we snow skied on Thursdays since lift tickets were free. During the three-hour drive to the

> *Though our schooling has been home-centered, we definitely haven't spent much time at home.*

slopes, the boys worked on school assignments. When we arrived, their brother John would join us since he attended college nearby. I told John he didn't have to ski with us since he could go anytime, but he just said, "It's fun!" John is an excellent skier and blessed his brothers by teaching them to ski. He had David jumping little ramps on his second day of skiing. When the slopes closed, we would eat dinner, buy John and his roommate some groceries, and sleep at their apartment.

Notice the "high" cost — free lift tickets and no hotel. We couldn't have afforded skiing if we had had to pay exorbitant weekend and holiday prices. Through the years, we have found evenings, weekends, and holidays a great time to work on academic assignments. Often, adventures and memorable activities have been available to us mid-week for a discount.

The most important thing I hope you glean from our story is that we love life and are passionate about living it with our children. Many years ago, a friend who is equally active with her seven children taught from the home told me a secret for enjoying my kids. She said, "I like being with my children because they obey me the first time I give an instruction."

> **The most important thing I hope you glean from our story is that we love life and we like being around our children.**

Our boys also are quick to obey. It only takes a hard look from their dad to let them know they are in trouble. Rob has never spanked them, but somehow they know he will if it serves their best interests. They know we want the best for them because we are always working together. Our children know our struggles, and we participate in their victories. We are there to support one another through life. We are not off in different directions for the better part of their childhood.

It is fun to see how quickly children grow from being hard work to helping hands. William wakes up and takes care of the dog and makes the family breakfast and lunch. Then he waters the plants. David cleans their bedroom, the bathrooms, and manages the trash. John comes home from his summer class at the community college and cleans the kitchen before working on the new addition to our house. Rob comes home from golfing and does laundry and makes a grocery list. I buy the groceries and put supper on the table. Many hands make light work.

For family recreation, we choose to do physical labor. In one summer, John and William trimmed out the garage door and painted it. The five of us worked on digging out a 20-by-12-by-1-foot pit, laying railroad ties, and hauling five cubic yards of sand to make a beach for our lake house. We eat each day in the sunroom addition John built with William and his dad as his helpers. David helped John build a garden wall. William helped me transform a rusted wrought iron table set into a beautifully sanded and painted piece of art. We end our days by fishing and swimming together. A full moon in winter signifies a picnic dinner in the dark followed by marshmallows and campfires.

For community outreach, we have lots of parties. It is so unfair that we get to live on our beautiful lake without you. So we have neighbors, church members, and home schooling families over just about every week during the summer. God has given us a fleet of small boats for free, and our off-lake neighbors are welcome to leave their boats tied to our bulkhead. Our backyard looks like a marina. When we first moved in, I was worried our retired neighbors with their pristine yards and empty docks would be angry with us. But each has made a point to come over and tell me how much they delight in seeing all the children use the lake.

For school, we spend a lot of time talking and thinking together. We wake up reading the Bible and go to bed reading good books. We get excited by the turtles that eat our fish bait, the frogs that live on our patio, and the antics of our crazy dog. Our newest adventure is learning to make videos of the boys' academic recitations to place on the Internet. William can produce an entire segment by himself now. An hour of math studies each day (two in the summer) keeps us moving ahead in a much-needed discipline.

The rewards of our passion for loving life and learning are many. A few come to mind. One night when John was 17 years old, I picked him up from work knowing he was anxious to go out with some friends. When he jumped into the car he said, "Mom, let's drive towards town. I want to take you to see the fireworks over the baseball stadium." He told me his friends could wait. Another time I was driving in the car when John yelled, "Stop! Pull over!" He proceeded to jump onto the hood with his cell phone so he could take a picture of a beautiful sunset. Currently, when he comes in from fishing at night, he brings his catch to show the family before he releases it. Our life is beautiful because of John.

Robert brings adventure. Due to his work, his travels as a rugby player, his enormously devoted friends around the country, and his desire to be an investor, we never know where he will be or what new thing he'll be involved in. Although he is grown, he always phones home to get our opinion first. I remember one time he called to tell me he had just made the winning "try" (rugby word for point) and his team was moving on to some higher level. It was very noisy, so I asked where he was. He said, "I'm standing in the end zone!" He had all of his college teammates jumping around and screaming, yet he called home to share the good news.

Unlike the media portrayal of rebellious teens, our two older boys actually liked being with their parents. Now as men, they choose to remain in close contact with us. We have moved from parents, to advisors, to friends that share in the passions of our grown children's lives. If you are considering teaching your children from home, it will not make your days any easier, but it could allow more of God's laughter to permeate your family's passion to love life and learning together. The passion to learn all God has revealed (and hidden) in His creation keeps the joy of living and learning alive in our home.

[1] Jamison, Kay Redfield 2005 *Exuberance: The Passion for Life* Vintage

Echo In Celebration

Chapter Two

The Cornerstone: Considering Home-Centered Education

"The only people who achieve much are those who want knowledge so badly that they seek it while the conditions are still unfavourable. Favourable conditions never come."
—C.S. Lewis

The cornerstone of home-centered education is, of course, the home, even more specifically the family and the Lord. This book was very hard for me to write. Parenting reminds me daily how short I fall of deserving God's blessings and how often I am just plain disobedient to His will. In many ways, I feel unqualified to even suggest that someone follow the model our family has adopted. You might fall short many times, just like I do, this is humbling and should keep us dependent upon the Lord for our adequacy (2 Cor 3:5). Yet I'm compelled to beg you: Compare the awful statistics facing the children of America today with the incredible, even miraculous, potential of a child raised to know his God-given talents and use them in a lifetime of service to Christ. Then consider what I call Home-Centered Education.

Raising children necessitates sacrificial labor and requires an attitude of constant prayer. Nothing I suggest in this book is easy. A friend and colleague of mine, Pastor Dru Dodson, asked that I not write this book promoting an overly simplistic "plug-in and play" concept that really helps no one. The "how-to" of educating our children wisely in today's technological and global world is complex; it cannot be reduced to a simple 1-2-3-step formula. In reality, the responsibility for the education and maturation of a handful of children is a scary thought. But as Teddy Roosevelt reminds us, we can't keep company with the timid and achieve greatness. (See Chap. 1, this book.)

One thing I know: Every single parent on this earth is capable of raising children in the knowledge and admonition of the Lord. Why? Because He commands it of us in Ephesians 6. And the Lord is trustworthy. He will not command us to do things we cannot do. He recognizes our failures, yet continues to trust us and entrust to us our children. He tells me, not the theologically trained divinity graduate, to walk with my children and teach them His commandments. He has given us the responsibility to make sure this task is being completed in a way that glorifies Him and builds up the body of Christ. As Robert Dabney, a Civil War pastor explains, "it is the Church's duty to instruct parents how God would have them rear their children, and enforce the duty by spiritual sanctions; but there its official power ends. It does not usurp the doing of the important task it inculcates." [1]

> *Raising children necessitates sacrificial labor and requires an attitude of constant prayer*

In Dabney's same essay, he goes on to explain how we can't expect Christian fruit from a secular tree. Even the best secular academic institution is not going to equip my sons to be ambassadors for Christ and to pass on the things He has done for us.

On the other hand, God hasn't equipped me or any parent to handle every aspect of a child's education and training. So we must rely on others to help in different ways during different seasons of our lives. Parents must help each other.

Therefore, to successfully facilitate your child's learning years, I propose that you consider Home-Centered Education. A Home-Centered Education is one that searches for the middle ground between solitary, do-it-yourself home schooling and an institutionalized education where parents relinquish all choices regarding their child's education. With Home-Centered Education, there may be years that you tackle the hard job of home schooling alone and other years when a tutor or a computer is utilized for a greater percentage of your children's education. Students may participate in some small groups, some large groups, and some individual learning situations. It is a flexible approach, able to bend toward the needs and desires of family life while providing ample opportunity for each student to pursue individual interests, thus creating an atmosphere where families love living and learning together.

> *Not that we are adequate in ourselves to consider anything as coming from ourselves, but our adequacy is from God, 2 Cor 3:5*

Beyond God's call to raise our children in the knowledge of Him, I see three forces in today's world driving American adults to consider Home-Centered Education: (1) government-run schools are not educating our children; (2) global technology is changing our world; (3) the successful home school movement is maturing. Examining these three things, I hope to inspire you to consider the new directions education is taking and make wise choices regarding your child's learning.

Force #1:
Government-run schools are not educating our children

Neil Postman, in his 1985 book *Amusing Ourselves to Death*, asserted that the age of show business has made it unnecessary to ban books — no one even wants to read books anymore. He argued that our love for the "technologies that undo our capacity to think" has resulted in a culture that has lost its appetite and subsequently its ability to process difficult ideas or large quantities of information. He prophetically assessed our current educational predicament well, since entertainment and pleasurable distractions are plentiful today.[2]

One reason why America's public schools are no longer educating our children is because modern, entertainment-driven educational techniques have left everyone confused about the true nature of education.

According to Peter Drucker in *The Post-Capitalist Society*, another reason institutional schools fail is because they are

> *Parents are actively seeking new, serious educational options in a wider range of prices and models to choose from.*

being asked to do two tasks they cannot do: (1) strengthen weaknesses rather than identify and strengthen gifts; and (2) socialize rather than teach.[3] Family, church and communities are designed for socializing. Schools should not be expected to replace the family or the church. In 2007, columnist Charles Davenport, Jr. rebuked Terry Grier, superintendent of the public schools in Guilford County, NC, because Grier listed the system's core values as "diversity, empathy, equality, innovativeness, and integrity" instead of reading, writing, and arithmetic.[4]

Educators are rightly concerned over the high rates of illiteracy. Our high school students are not preparing to be global leaders. Parents now want some new, serious educational options in a wider range of prices and models to choose from. Free education has proven to mean the same as a free lunch, there just "ain't" no such thing. As Linda Cannell said in a discussion with a Doctorate of Ministry class on global church-based theological education, "Schools are our most educationally impoverished institutions." (March 10, 2006, Gordon Conwell Theological Seminary, MA)

Many parents, particularly those whose children are enrolled in elite private schools, may conclude that I don't know what I am talking about as their kids are "just fine, thank-you. Those illiteracy statistics must be for some other area of town." My response is that their standards of literacy are too low. If you disagree with me, please stop and read the following paragraph from Thomas Paine's "Common Sense."

> *"Thus necessity, like a gravitating power, would soon form our newly arrived emigrants into society, the reciprocal blessings of which would supersede, and render the obligations of law and government unnecessary while they remained perfectly just to each other; but as nothing but Heaven is impregnable to vice, it will unavoidably happen that in proportion as they surmount the first difficulties of emigration, which bound them together in a common cause, they will begin to relax in their duty and attachment to each other: and this remissness will point out the necessity of establishing some form of government to supply the defect of moral virtue."*[5]

Paine's pamphlet was written to be readable by the average 12 year old in Colonial America. Few modern adults, let alone a sixth grader, can read this document well enough to explain its arguments and conclusions to another adult. Parents need to recognize that our current literacy standards are very low. An interesting aside is that over half the people who purchased "Common Sense" were either indentured servants or African slaves.

A talkative gentleman at my gym approached me one day and said, "Do you know how we make fun of the employees at McDonald's because they don't know how to make change without the register telling them what to do? Well, my daughter just got a job running a cash register. She came home crying from work the first day because she realized she doesn't know how to make change. She is a straight-A senior at the local public high school. How did

---

The State of Education in the US[6]

According to the government's own statistics:

☉ In 2004, China graduated 500,000 engineers, and India graduated 200,000 while the United States graduated only 70,000 engineers.

☉ Until the 1950s education cost practically nothing, and the US had a literacy rate of 90% or better. Today, the District of Columbia spends over $13,000 a year per student, and

☉ Less than 50% of American high school students graduate as proficient readers.

☉ Less than 15% of American high school students graduate as proficient mathematicians.

☉ In 2006, only 60% of high school seniors graduated.

---

this happen?" We had never spoken before, and he had no idea who I was. I told him that his story wasn't unusual and that I home schooled. He told me his wife home schooled when their children were younger and then they went to an elite, private school in the Bahamas until they went to an American public high school. This caring family discovered that doing well in school is not the same as being educated.

Force #2:

Global technology is changing our world

New technologies, when used appropriately, have also ripened the ground for Home-Centered Education. Technology has made it possible to work and learn "from home." Charles Handy, author of *The Age of Unreason*, points out:

> "From home is different than at home. The home is the base not the prison. We can leave it. There will be organized work clubs, work centers, meeting rooms, and conference centers.... It is not a lonely life." (p. 178)[7]

Technocrats and entrepreneurs daily use computers to start companies and to take courses in conjunction with citizens all around the globe. Many adults now work wherever they like thanks to wireless Internet. As well, the home serves as a valuable, low-cost center for post-secondary education via online universities and distance learning courses. One day, it will be possible to have a 3-D image of a great math professor from another continent stand in your living room and tutor your family. These changes should encourage us to get comfortable using technology to learn and to work and also to take advantage of opportunities to instruct our children through computers. Wireless technology has given adults the world as a classroom. Why shouldn't our children have the same advantages?

As these new technologies bring exciting changes to our world, we should look to the future and anticipate different trends in employment and economic opportunities. Home-Centered Education encourages learning for the sake of loving life, and one key aspect of that philosophy is being prepared to enjoy hard work done well. I know I want my boys equipped to provide well for my grandchildren, their church, and the local community through a variety of careers and adventures. So it is important for me to understand what's ahead for them.

> *Technology is rapidly changing the landscape of employment, and therefore education.*

Technology and globalism are rapidly changing the landscape of employment and, therefore, education. In fact, analysts predict the very idea of a lifelong career will disappear and we will revert back to the pre-industrial era idea of work being made up of a series of tasks and jobs throughout our lives.

Institutionalized, government-mandated schooling is an anomaly in the history of education and a result of the need for daycare through the industrial era. Before the U.S. Civil War, everyone farmed and worked from home or within their community. In the wireless age, adults are returning to the home and are becoming more flexible than ever. Even if they choose to remain in offices for cost, for social, or for productivity reasons, all adults will be continually trained through computer technology. Even if you are only training yourself to pursuing personal interests online, you are still learning new ways to use computers.

Taken as a whole, these new working conditions, the ready access to technology, the ease of learning using computers, and the desire for effective, low-cost educational models have all inspired more families to investigate Home-Centered Education. More than ever, it is feasible, even desirable, to teach "from home."

My older boys already take online college courses within their university setting, I'm studying for my doctorate through a distance learning program, and our family owns an Internet company. The world's experts and resources are ours. For active, engaged learners, sitting in the same building for the better part of their childhood portrays an artificial view of today's world. The same would be true

Technology and Home-Centered Education

☞ More than 75 percent of the labor force in the most industrialized nations engages in work that is little more than simple repetitive tasks.

In the United States alone, that means in the years ahead more than 90 million jobs in the labor force of 124 million are potentially vulnerable to replacement by machines.

Home-Centered Education for adults is endorsed by many leading futurists due to inexpensive access to expanding technologies. (Jeremy Rifkin. *The End of Work: The Decline of the Global Labor Force and the Dawn of the Post-Market Era.* New York: G.P. Putman's Sons, 1995 pp. xvi-xvii)

☞ By some estimates, one-quarter of the working population will be working from home by the end of the century. (Charles Handy *The Age of Unreason* Boston: Harvard Business School Press, 1989 p. 178)

☞ Twenty-eight point seven (28.7) million Americans have worked from home at least one day a month. Thirty-nine percent (39%) of Americans say they would rather telecommute than drive to a main office. (International Telework Association and Council, February 2007)

☞ Thirteen percent (13%) of employees check their business e-mail while on vacation. ("Might As Well Face it... We're Addicted to E-mail" AOL, 2005)

if students just sat at home with books or computers and called it Home-Centered Education. Our home has been but the base for many learning opportunities, and I only see those opportunities expanding in our increasingly technological world.

Force #3:
The successful home school movement is maturing

The third force driving the rise of Home-Centered Education is the success of home schooling. Home schooling has grown from a fringe movement to a serious option for families concerned about their children's education. Millions of American parents have been successfully educating their own children for the last 25 years, and so, an army of home schooling pioneers is now available to help guide and support new parents considering Home-Centered Education.

These experienced families are eager to take all they've learned to their community, often while supplementing their own family's income. Schools, churches, and individual families have begun to greatly value the knowledge successful home schoolers bring to their community. The educational community should enthusiastically welcome these talented adults to share what they've learned. My own experience has been that parents who would never consider home schooling will do so if they can depend on continual support from an experienced mentor in this challenging endeavor.

Unfortunately, home schooling is often thought of as nothing more than "school at home." The term doesn't communicate a different model of education than what you would find in an institutional school and doesn't necessarily inspire the idea of loving life and learning together. Thus I prefer the term Home-Centered Education. I don't want my children to associate education with an institution or system. I want them to be curious about learning everywhere and to eagerly seek conversations with others who are passionate about life. This is how my children find mentors and grow beyond our family's limitations.

Millions of American parents have been successfully educating their own children for the last twenty-five years.

At my older sons' graduation ceremonies, we chose to honor the men who were major influences in their lives. We had celebratory feasts in our backyard where we invited the men to come on the stage (it was an old halfpipe for skateboarding) and speak about the graduate so our extended family, church members, neighbors, and friends would know that we had not educated them alone. We actively pursued other adults' help. Home is the center of our life but not the focus of our life. Serving others and growing in the grace and favor of God and men is our focus. That requires excellent academics, extensive life skills, and a love for adventure.

The failure of government schools to educate our kids, the changes wrought by expanding technologies, and the successes of pioneer home schoolers can only lead to greater growth in the movement that I call Home-Centered Education. Some parents will continue to home school like we early pioneers without much help from anyone. Some will not teach at all and will sit their child in front of a machine, like a computer or TV, for a good portion of the day. I suspect most will choose a middle road. They will use technology to find the best, most interesting and most current information. They will spend time and money on support services delivered by home schooling pioneers.

And they will love living and learning themselves while they study together with their children.

By working together, intentional parents can create a hybrid of home schooling and an academic resource center. They can take advantage of the knowledge of successful home educators while using inexpensive technologies to bring great learning content into their homes. They can utilize experienced home school tutors in group settings while forming co-ops for activities like sports and fine arts. The home will once again become the center of a child's education just as it is becoming the center of the adult work world. Americans are not going back to the farm, but we do have an opportunity to go back to the home as the most nurturing place to disciple our children in the love of life and learning.

Home-Centered Education

I've been blessed to be part of a large Home-Centered Education community full of parents teaching their children to love life and learning. These parents embrace living. Like Teddy Roosevelt, they believe life is the "unpacking of endless Christmas stockings."[9] (Miller, p. 237) They believe that, if practiced a lot, it is possible to pass the sacrificial love of God and family to the younger generation. And they persevere to learn in spite of poor resources and less than favorable conditions, because, as C.S. Lewis remarked, "favourable conditions never come." These parents also yearn to show other parents how to teach their children to find the "joy (that) widens one's view of the world and expands imaginative thought. (Joy) activates. It makes both physical and intellectual exploration more likely, and it provides reward for problems solved or risks taken."[10]

So, let's be creative and brainstorm new possibilities.

A culture of learning occurs when parents know and behave as though they, and not a school principal or headmaster, are responsible for their child's education. As I said earlier, I am not proposing a simplistic formula for anyone as every family situation is different. I am proposing an idealistic goal, and then, I hope you will actively direct and take responsibility for your child's education. Home-Centered Education will be more difficult for some families than for others. No matter how "unfavourable the conditions," you have the exciting task of discovering your children's gifts while challenging them to apply their strengths and the Lord's power to overcoming weaknesses. It is very hard work to wisely direct children's curiosity while guiding them to love to live a God-centered life. Did I say it was very hard? I'll say it again. It is very hard work to disciple a child's heart, mind, and soul to love the Lord and his or her neighbor. But it is a work you can love and love sharing. It is redemptive work, because it demonstrates to your children that they are more than just consumers called "students;" they are creatures made in God's image and they are worthy of sacrifice.

A culture of learning occurs when parents know and behave as though they, and not a school principal or headmaster, are responsible for their child's education.

One day, a neighbor approached me while I was doing lawn work. He wanted to encourage me to keep home schooling. I knew nothing about this retired gentleman's family, so he told me that he and his wife and all of their grown children were involved as teachers in school systems. He had had a recent call with a very frustrated daughter who spent most of her days in court as an ombudsman for her students instead of in the classroom as their teacher. He was lamenting about how different school was since he and his wife had taught.

I asked him, "You consider yourself to be a Christian man, correct? How in the world did your generation think that if we handed the greater portion of our children's lives over to the state that they would bear Christian fruit? The Bible tells us our foundation is the Rock. Anything else is sinking sand." He replied, "We just never thought about it."

I called this chapter The Cornerstone because, as parents, we need to think about what anchors our lives. Scripture calls Jesus the Rock, the Cornerstone. He is the only sure foundation for anything in all of life. He needs to be the cornerstone of living, of loving, and of learning. We should anchor our children's education to his teachings. For many, a Home-Centered Education that works from the home, utilizes modern technologies, and builds on the success of the home school movement is rapidly becoming the most desirable way to accomplish this God-given task. He is the only sure foundation for any form of education, the parents are the primary stewards of their children's education, and the home is center from which His world becomes the classroom.

[1] Dabney, Robert, *Securalized Education* Retrieved Aug. 2006 from the World Wide Web: http://wellingtonchristianschools.org.nz/dabney.pdf

[2] Postman, Neil 1985 *Amusing Ourselves to Death* The Penguin Group

[3] Drucker, Peter 1994 *The Post-Capitalist Society* Harper Collins

[4] Davenport Jr., Charles June 24, 2007 *Greensboro News & Record*, quoting Grier, Terry *Guilford Co. School's Back to School Guide* 2007 Retrieved from the World Wide Web: http://www.guilford.k12.nc.us/parents/pdf/back to schoolguide-2007_graphic.pdf

[5] Paine, Thomas Retrieved Aug. 2006 from the World Wide Web at http://www.ushistory.org/PAINE/commonsense/singlehtml.htm

[6] National Assessment of Educational Progress (NAEP) Retrieved Aug. 2006 from the World Wide Web at http:nces.ed.gov/nationsreportcard/

[7] Handy, Charles 1998 *The Age of Unreason*, 1st Edition Harvard Business School Press

[9] Miller, Nathan 1994 *Theodore Roosevelt* Harper Collins

[10] Jamison, Kay Redfield 2005 *Exuberance: The Passion for Life* Vintage

Chapter Three

The History: Pondering Literacy and Education

"The first book of Kings tell us that (Solomon) studied biology (both animal and plant life), wrote over a thousand songs, and collected three thousand proverbs from sources in the ancient world. Ecclesiastes indicates that he weighed and studied these proverbs and arranged them in order. That he sought 'pleasing words' as well as words of truth indicates his concern about the aesthetic. Foreign rulers came to him for advice, and his decision making amazed them. He invested in international commerce and spurred the economic development of his country...Solomon's name has stood through three millennia for wisdom, its importance, its social application, and its divine source."
—Holmes, *Building the Christian Academy*, p. 3

D uring my 20-plus years as an active learner, I've realized that I just don't know that much and I want to know a lot more. I could have been self-satisfied and impressed with my aerospace engineering degree and made a decent income. The world said I was educated. Huh! It lied! I couldn't comprehend the French in *Henry V*, the Latin in *National Review Magazine*, or *The Federalist Papers* in English. Yet any 14 year old could have done so

240 years ago in the American colonies. When I graduated from college, I couldn't tell you a single constellation, the name of an African country or an Australian province. I couldn't tell you what century Charles Martel, Pepin the Short and Charlemagne lived in nor that they were related to one another, nor what countries

> *If I am going to ensure my children are effectively educated, I need to look at models that are proven to work instead of repeating the ineffective methods I was taught.*

they ruled. I was highly literate and very uneducated.

If I am going to ensure my children are effectively educated, I need to look at models that are proven to work instead of repeating the ineffective methods I was taught. The only time in the recorded history of this planet that we have had universal literacy was in the U.S. from 1605 to the 1950s.

All other cultures before and since have been significantly less literate or purely oral. So I want to know: What did the average parent and teacher do to raise the most literate nation ever? And I want to develop our family's educational model in light of that knowledge.

In his book *Amusing Ourselves to Death*, Neil Postman analyzes literacy rates from the Colonial era through the 1900s.

> *"And although literacy rates are notoriously difficult to assess, there is sufficient evidence that between 1640 and 1700, the literacy rate for men in Massachusetts and Connecticut was somewhere between 89 and 95 percent… The literacy rate for women is estimated to run as high as 62 percent in the years 1681-1697."*(p.31)[1]

He proceeds to give details of the American Lyceum movement throughout the 1800s, about which Alfred Bunn, a visiting Englishman, remarked, *"It is a matter of wonderment... to witness the youthful workmen, the over-tired artisan, the worn-out factory girl... rushing... after the toil of the day is over, into the hot atmosphere of the over-crowded lecture room"* (p.40) to hear intellectuals speak for hours.

Postman details the numbers of various copies of books sold in cities as a percent of the population, proving that every adult bought books and read.

An Older Standard of Literacy

I am so intrigued by the educational levels of these average early Americans compared to average modern Americans. We are told they were mostly unschooled, which is true, but then we are left to conclude that they were uneducated, which is not true. They were far better educated than modern children. As illustration, read this passage from popular literature.

Rebecca of SunnyBrook Farm, published in 1903, contains a conversation between Miss Dearborn, an 18-year-old country schoolteacher, and her student, Rebecca.

> [Miss Dearborn:] "Now let's have our conjugations. Give me the verb 'to be', potential mood, past perfect tense."
> [Rebecca:]" I might have been
> Thou mightst have been
> He might have been
> We might have been
> You might have been
> They might have been."
>   "Give me an example, please."

"I might have been glad. Thou mightst have been glad. He, she, or it might have been glad."

"'He' or 'she' might have been glad because they are masculine and feminine, but could 'it' have been glad?" asked Miss Dearborn, who was very fond of splitting hairs.

"Why not?" asked Rebecca.

"Because 'it' is neuter gender."

"Couldn't we say, 'The kitten might have been glad if it had known it was not going to be drowned'?"

"Ye—es," Miss Dearborn answered hesitatingly, never very sure of herself under Rebecca's fire; "but though we often speak of a baby, a chicken, or a kitten as 'it,' they are really masculine or feminine gender, not neuter."

Rebecca reflected a long moment and then asked, "Is a hollyhock neuter?"

"Oh, yes, of course it is, Rebecca."

"Well, couldn't we say, 'The hollyhock might have been glad to see the rain, but there was a weak little hollyhock bud growing out of its stalk and it was afraid that it might be hurt by the storm; so the big hollyhock was kind of afraid, instead of being real glad'?"

Miss Dearborn looked puzzled as she answered, "Of course, Rebecca, hollyhocks could not be sorry, or glad, or afraid, really."

We can't tell, I s'pose," replied the child; "but I think they are, anyway. Now, what shall I say?" [2]

Even though Rebecca is fictional, the author wrote the book with the expectation that nine-year-old girls would be able to appreciate Rebecca's conjugating experience. Americans today don't even know what it means to conjugate a verb, let alone be able to do so. When they learn what it means they think they are "fine" because they get along quite well without knowing how to conjugate verbs. Yet verb conjugations are the basis for any sentence structure in any language.

There are lots of difficult issues to resolve with globalization, but the ability to learn a foreign language should not be one of them in an educated culture. We should know the tools of how to learn to conjugate verbs in any language. Just as Colonial students were expected to master Greek and Hebrew and Latin in high school, we should expect our students to master Spanish, Chinese, and Arabic.

In Colonial Heights, south of Richmond, Va., the public schools have students who speak Spanish, Korean, Vietnamese, and Mandarin.

> *"Knowing one language doesn't even prepare (the teacher),' said Kerry Robinson, director of Instructional Administration. The U.S. has a shortage of teachers, so the U.S. Departments of Defense and Education have teamed up to train retiring military personnel to be tomorrow's school teachers through the Troops to Teachers (TTT) program. American teachers speaking Mandarin? Retired soldiers receiving bonuses to teach? Parents must really think in new ways in order to prepare their children for a world very different from the 20th century."* The Patriot, Vol. 4, No. 23, Feb. 16, 2007.

Ralph Moody wrote an incredibly inspiring, autobiographical series of non-fiction books set during the same time period as Laura Ingalls Wilder's *Little House* series. In *Mary Emma and Company*, Ralph's family moves from the Colorado frontier of one-room schoolhouses to the public school system of Boston. He has to take an elementary placement test so the principal knows where to put him.

"Mr. Jackson didn't let her [Ralph's mother, Mary Emma] finish, but looked down at me and asked, 'What is the result of twelve times twelve, divided by thirteen, times five, divided by three?' I got along all right until I came to fifty-five and five-thirteenths, then I got a little bit mixed up in trying to divide it by three, and Mr. Jackson mixed me up more by saying, 'Come, come, boy! What is the answer?'

'I don't know,' I told him. 'I got mixed up when I got into the thirteenths…'" [3]

Ralph had the correct answer except for the final step of dividing by three. And so, Ralph was placed in seventh grade. How many of today's adults can hold that many numbers and operations in their head? Yet it was commonly expected of all children a century ago, as evidenced by the standard math text of that period, *Ray's Higher Arithmetic*, published in 1880 by Van Antwerp, Bragg, & Co.

> *Today, in the US, most children have lots of teachers, lots of subjects, lots of activities, lots of money, and yet they learn comparatively little.*

In U.S. schools today, most children have lots of teachers, lots of subjects, lots of activities and lots of money, yet they learn comparatively little. Modern middle and high school consists of six or more subjects taught by six or more teachers. The students don't know the goal of each subject, are never given an overview of the particulars of an individual subject let alone how it relates to other subjects, and don't get the time needed to fall in love with a trusted teacher before they are shuffled off to another classroom or grade. Teachers rightly resent having to teach to a standardized multiple choice test instead of teaching how to learn.

Remember that before 1950, the proficient literacy rate in this country was about 90 percent and had been so since before the Colonial period. As of 2006, it is about 50 percent.[1] We certainly have children in school buildings for more years, longer hours, and with more money, yet here I am as an adult trying to catch up with the eighth graders of 150 years ago. What happened?

> *We should know how to learn to conjugate verbs in any language, just as colonial students were expected to master Greek and Hebrew and Latin in high school, we should expect our students to master Spanish, Chinese, and Arabic.*

A friend told me a story that illustrates why we are in so much academic trouble and why the tools of effective education have been lost.

There once was a cage that held four gorillas. In the middle of the cage was a box. Every morning, the zookeeper hung beautifully fresh bananas above the box, and the gorillas climbed the box to get the bananas. One morning, the first gorilla climbed the box, and as soon as he was atop, fire hoses shot out of the walls and painfully pummeled all four of the creatures. A few minutes later, another gorilla climbed the box and the same thing happened. A few tries more, and the gorillas decided the bananas weren't worth the pain that day. After a few days of the same, they quit even trying to climb the box. If one of the gorillas forgot and started even looking at those beautiful bananas, the other gorillas would gang up and beat him. Eventually, the poor beasts never approached the box or looked at the bananas. Then the zookeeper replaced one of the gorillas. The new gorilla was so excited when he saw the box and the bananas. As he swung his long arm toward the box the other three gorillas pummeled him while screaming. He hung his head and ran to a corner. Every morning, as he got excited over the fresh bananas, the other gorillas began the torture. Once that gorilla was trained to stay away from the box, the zookeeper substituted another new gorilla. He repeated substitutions until all four of the original gorillas that had been painfully hosed were gone and there were four new gorillas. The new gorillas had never been hosed, but they continued to beat each other if anyone went for the box and bananas. They had no idea why they did what they did, but it was all they knew so they continued.

Slowly but surely in American schools over the past century, excellent teachers who knew how to teach have been beaten down by a system that demanded they socialize instead of educate children. Today's teachers have no idea how much students used to learn, how the students were successfully taught, or why the changes in academics were made. The teachers want to do what is right, but they're not sure what "right" is.

As a result, most public schools merely lead students through a survey of a variety of subjects, hoping somehow a subject may become relevant or understood. They choose to spend lots of time and money on "character education," while our literacy rate has dropped from 90 to 50 percent.

Studying the Tools of Learning

I entered adulthood with an inadequate education, even though I was a voracious reader, and had the support of parents who loved to challenge me. I was accepted at the University of Michigan College of Engineering thanks to affirmative action. They wanted female engineers, and I was one of the few who wanted to study aerospace engineering. My father was pleased that I chose his alma mater even though I had a full scholarship to another university. It

> *I hadn't learned to struggle with thoughts that were complex and make them my own. I hadn't been taught how to teach myself something new.*

was fun to go through the original Michigan engineering building and see pictures of my father and grandfather when the school was so much smaller.

But what wasn't fun was my inability to study. High school was easy. I hadn't learned to struggle with thoughts that were complex and make them my own. I hadn't been taught how to teach myself something new. I hadn't been required to do a lot of memorizing and wrestling with ideas so I could understand and apply basic concepts to complex situations.

Studying math and science in college was very hard for me. I liked what I was learning; I just wasn't very good at it. The only redeeming feature I had was that I had enough sense to join study groups and to look for help.

In a moment that changed my life forever, someone showed me what I was doing wrong. One of my study partners found learning easy. He was helping me with a problem when, in frustration, he slammed the very heavy text I was using onto my hand and said, "Stop trying to find the answer and start trying to understand the problem!"

Well, that was a new thought! In high school, I just knew the answer and got A's. How was I to do this? The first thing he told me was revolutionary. If the question is in the book, that means the answer is in the material. Really? I thought if I didn't "get it" by just reading the book that meant the author hadn't explained the problem very well. He proceeded to show me how to read graphs and pictures and text to get information. He showed me how to step through each problem analyzing every fact and pattern and algorithm. He showed me how to make up my own problems just like the text's examples to make sure I understood what was taught. In other words, he began to teach me how to think. I thought you just read the text and tried to answer the problem. I didn't know you had to wrestle with the concepts and make them your own. I thought if it wasn't easy it was the book's fault or the teacher's fault. Fortunately, my husband, who I met the next year, also knew how to study and continued to help me. It was so nice to go from a C average to a B average in my engineering courses and even get some A's.

When I decided to home school my boys, I began to prepare myself to teach. I wanted to help them avoid the mistakes I had made. I took classes on how to teach math. I worked through phonics and handwriting and Latin books. I went to home schooling and parenting conferences. I joined home school support groups. I lead science and math clubs. I took the boys on field trips. I did everything you can think of to be a good teacher.

What I didn't know was the only thing I was preparing for was a repeat of the poor education I had received. I was preparing to teach my boys to survey content instead of how to learn any content from any source. I didn't have the maturity or experience at that point to analyze why my education was so poor. I was determined that somehow there had to be a better way to educate my boys, but I didn't know what that looked like. As other home schooling pioneers have said, we were the worst bunch of home schoolers ever! We had no mentors. We had no knowledge of effective educational methods. We knew only the same "survey the text and shuffle to the next class" techniques that we had been taught.

> *Because I was not taught the tools of learning in school, I was ill-equipped to pass effective educational tools onto my own two sons.*

Because I was not taught the tools of learning in school, I was ill-equipped to pass effective educational tools onto my own two sons. I loved my boys and I wanted the best for them, but my "gorillas" taught me lessons that were disconnected from a heritage when American schools were effective. I was probably able to do a better job than many parents since I liked reading and I had struggled with teaching myself to learn some difficult material. But I had no one to mentor me as I broke down the process of learning into manageable steps for each of my children's unique developmental levels. I read a lot of books that tried to be helpful, but much of the methodology was just wrong.

In the 1980s, there was a serious public cry from conservatives for a return to the "basics" that was mocked by progressives. Despite good intentions from parents, teachers, and administrators, nothing much happened. There were and continue to be occasional success stories among charter and private schools and definite successes achieved within individual classrooms, but overall, academic skills we can measure haven't improved. I think it is because the folks crying out for the basics didn't really know quite what they meant. The teachers who knew how to teach had retired. Modern experimentalists had taken over the teaching colleges and weren't interested in what had worked in the past.

While teaching educators how to teach, I've realized that we make too light a matter of little things and don't spend enough time defining the basics. In 1995, I taught in a Jamaican Christian mission school for two weeks. When I first walked into the classroom, I was appalled at the assignments given to the first graders. The six year olds sat each morning for about an hour copying, in cursive, a long Scripture passage from the board. As they did so, the teacher worked individually with a few remedial students. All I could think was, "How boring."

It seemed like such busy work when there were so many interesting things to cover. But by the end of my two weeks, I began to see they were right and I was wrong. What I witnessed was the same method that had been used forever, but was foreign to me as a modern.

I realized the tools of learning these children were being given, and I've spent the time since pondering their methods and trying to imitate their results.

- All of them could sit quietly for a long time.
- All of them could read every word.
- All of them had memorized lots of Scripture.
- All of them had the fine motor skills required to look up at a board and replicate the work on a piece of paper.
- All of them had the hand strength to hold their pencil properly and for a long time.
- All of them had beautiful handwriting.

Don't Make Light of Small Things

Let's examine these basics more thoroughly.

Self-control: *All of them could sit quietly for a long time*.

Teaching children self-control allows them to study and listen and think for longer periods of time. If this is difficult for your children, their bodies need to be trained. If they can sit and watch TV, you know they are physically capable of self-control. They may have to be mentally trained to sit when they are not so intensely engaged. Begin with five minutes a day and increase the time they can sit until they are used to sitting still for a certain amount of time each day.

Literacy: *All of them could read every word.*
Reading the same small amount of material builds speed and accuracy that moves students to higher levels of literacy.

Memorization: *All of them had memorized lots of Scripture.* Copying Scripture is one of many tools we use to memorize God's Word for the times we want to rejoice or need strength.

Concentration: *All of them had the fine motor skills required to look up at a board and replicate the work on a piece of paper.* This is very hard for a young child. Tracking images and reproducing them in another medium develops physical control and trains the brain to hold ideas.

Coordination: *All of them had the hand strength to hold their pencil properly and for a long time.* Currently schools employ physical therapists to teach children to strengthen their hands to hold their pencils. Long gone are the days of butter churning and bread kneading.

Patience: *All of them had beautiful handwriting.* Though no longer important for communication since the advent of the keyboard, handwriting practice still teaches students to develop an artistic eye and an eye for detail.

Copy work is the tool used to develop all of the above skills. Art and fine motor control go hand-in-hand. Anything children can copy beautifully teaches them patience and pride in a job well done.

My older elementary children could do none of these things well, but they sure knew how to have fun! The self-discipline trained into the Jamaican children gave them the basic skills needed for everything else they would ever study in any situation. I was pregnant at the time and knew my next child would be taught the skills I was witnessing. These children were very poor and had some of the same learning disabilities as all children, but no one was catering to their weaknesses. The tasks assigned were simple, thorough, and mastered by all of the children.

As I searched to identify the differences between educational successes of the past and the failure of current models, I realized I had seen the answers in that Jamaican classroom. Our nation's capital spends over $13,000 per student per year and is not educating its graduates. The Jamaican teachers spent pennies and were preparing their children well. They taught in a setting similar to the one-room schoolhouses that were so successful in our nation's past and with an expectation that the students would work hard with minimal resources. No teacher-prepared handouts. No computers that made things fun. Just students expecting a teacher to show them how to transfer information from her mind to theirs.

> *I discovered that effective educators and parents used to teach the art of learning, memorizing, and reciting grammar; hence, earlier schools were called Grammar Schools.*

Through my study of American education, I have discovered teaching techniques everyone, not just professional teachers, knew before the 1920s, yet have almost been lost since. Thank God for books that record the past and for cultural analysts like British authors Dorothy Sayers and C.S. Lewis who wrote about the errors in modern educational philosophies. I have discovered that effective educators and parents used to teach the art of learning, memorizing, and reciting grammar; hence, earlier schools were called grammar schools.

The goal of early American grammar schools was to teach children how to fill their brains with lots of information and practice retrieving it to prove they actually knew something. New students heard older students' recitations; older students reviewed previous years' memory work while listening to younger students' recitations. The methodology of repetition on paper, orally, and aurally met the needs of all learning styles and allowed one young teacher to instruct a lot of children of different ages and abilities at one time.

If you want to see this methodology done well today, watch an elementary school bandmaster. They have no choice but to use these techniques. They take a lot of students of all ages and abilities, instruct them to sit still for a long time while playing the same piece of music over and over, and magic happens. Everyone learns the musical composition, and they play as one. All subjects were effectively taught this way in early American grammar schools.

If we have any hope of restoring such a literate, well-educated culture, we must not capriciously repeat the educational model of the previous generation. Rather we must work to intentionally recover the standards and expectations that our students can learn how to learn — given the proper tools and inspiration.

[1] Postman, Neil 1985. *Amusing Ourselves to Death,* The Penguin Group.

[2] Wiggin, Kate Douglas 1910. *Rebecca of Sunnybrook, Farm* Grosset & Dunlap.

[3] Moody, Ralph 1994. *Mary Emma and Company,* Bison Books.

Echo In Celebration

Chapter Four

The Tools: Recovering the Classical Model

> *"Do you ever find that young people, when they have left school, not only forget most of what they have learned (that is only to be expected), but forget also, or betray that they have never really known, how to tackle a new subject for themselves?"*
> —Dorothy Sayers, *The Lost Tools of Learning*, 1947

In the 1990's, I was fortunate enough to read classical educator Doug Wilson's *Recovering the Lost Tools of Learning* around the same time that John Gatto, who quit teaching after winning NY Teacher of the Year, was writing books about the ineffective teaching techniques currently used in US schools. A glimmer, a very small ray of light hit my heart like a laser beam. I began to question all that I knew about learning. I began to recognize ingrained thoughts that were lies. I began to see how to use my natural learning strengths to bolster the areas where I was weak. I had a hope in my heart that I could teach Robert and John the study skills I had begun to learn, though I didn't understand them, in college. I began to understand why my husband and his peers, who are about ten years older than me, were

> *Every subject needs to be attacked by a student like a foreign language, for every subject has its own lingo, jargon, or grammar.*

better educated. I had always been a thinker, but now I had a new paradigm to push my thoughts through.

I learned that good teachers had always fully understood that learning any information is a three step process. As Dorothy Sayers describes it, I must first behave like a parrot, meaning that I practice repeating back basic vocabulary and ideas and concepts of something new. Every subject needs to be attacked by a student like a foreign language, for every subject has its own lingo, jargon, or grammar. For instance, I have been trying to learn about paper quality for the various materials my production company creates. I can't just order a bookmark and expect that the product I had in mind is what will arrive in the mail and was produced at the best price for the quality. I have to learn the names of various paper weights, paper glosses, laminate thicknesses, and different margin bleeds. I need to memorize the grammar of a printer. Once I understand what these terms mean, I can email a file to any printer on the Internet that has the best prices and send instructions like, "I want linen paper at 100 lb weight, 3-hole punched, double-sided, black and white, covered with a clear 2 mm laminate" and get what I want. Then I can teach someone else how to order bookmarks for me. If I can teach new ideas to others using the specific language of a subject, I am educated in that field. I have the skill to learn anything if I know how:

1. to memorize vocabulary and rules (also called grammar)
2. to process new concepts (also called dialectic)
3. to clearly explain the grammar and dialectic to others (also called rhetoric).

I apply the same thinking process to learning any new academic material. I look through a new chemistry chapter and read the relevant summary, glossary, bold-faced letters, pictures, and graphs trying to get a general grasp of what the author is going to say. Then I read through the chapter taking notes and using a dictionary. This is how I build my ability to read difficult or new ideas with understanding. The chapter will be hard for me to just read and enjoy if I don't understand the subject's basic vocabulary. These two exercises are often enough to make the content more meaningful and easier to read. Then I reread the chapter with a calculator in hand and work out any mathematical concepts or try any exercises. At this point, I am gaining understanding, and I am impressing the information to a place in my brain where I can retain and use it. Once the grammar is understood, I can just read that chapter's text with the ease of a novel and rework the math problems and demonstrate that I actually understand the material by taking a test or participating in a discussion. Tests and conversations are ways to clarify errors in thought so they can be restudied.

Together, these skills are referred to in Latin as the trivium, or the three roads - grammar, dialectic, and rhetoric - in classical education models. But those terms sound so academic that we often can't see how they apply beyond the study of English or writing. So let's rename these skills as:

- the ability to input information,
- the ability to process information,
- the ability to output information.

According to Scripture, we were designed to fill our brain with knowledge, understand its implications, and then use the information with wisdom.

By wisdom a house is built, and through understanding it is established; through knowledge its

rooms are filled with rare and beautiful treasures.
A wise man has great power, and a man of knowl-
edge increases strength. Proverbs 24: 3-5

Education through Grammar

"But first: what age shall the children be? Well, if one
is to educate them on novel lines, it will be better that
they should have nothing to unlearn; besides, one
cannot begin a good thing too early, and the Trivium
is by its nature not learning, but a preparation
for learning. We will, therefore, "catch 'em young,"
requiring of our pupils only that they shall be able to
read, write, and cipher."
—Dorothy Sayers, *The Lost Tools of Learning,* 1947

Grammar in 19th century dictionaries is defined as the science of vocabulary. Every new task, idea, or concept has a vocabulary that must be acquired like a foreign language before a student can progress to more difficult or abstract tasks within that body of knowledge. There is a science or system that the vocabulary defines, describes and organizes.

It's hard to evaluate an historian's analysis of world events if you don't know the names (the grammar) of the people and places and dates he's referring too. You can't analyze the "Why's" of history if you don't first know who, what, where, and when. It's hard to know if your car mechanic is dishonest or giving good advice if you can't decipher the grammar of his diagnosis. "The 'what' is rubbing against the 'which' when the cylinder pushes past the 'how' and you want $600?" Or say you're applying for your first home loan and you keep hearing words like "interest only", "variable rate", "amortized" and "Please sign here…" The interest only mortgage boom in the 2000's financially destroyed many families who didn't understand basic multiplication.

Every subject is like learning a foreign language until you have a basic grasp of vocabulary and the main ideas associated with the topic. This is called grammar — words and how they work together. Mathematicians have a special grammar; physicists have their own jargon; archeologists and cooks, dancers and musicians all have a 'lingo' they use. To learn something new, we must first try to discover the grammar that an expert in that field uses. So the first tool of learning is "Learn the Grammar."

How can we teach our children to do that? Let me begin with a view of the possible rather than the impossible. Let me prove to you that people are all geniuses, designed to store and manipulate large amounts of grammar. Imagine the grocery store you shop in. If I asked you to tell me where the eggs are so I could run right in and grab them, would you be able to do so? Of course you could. The average grocery store carries over 30,000 items and you can quickly tell me where to find most of them. Why? Because it is organized by category, and you have shopped in similar stores repeatedly. In other words, you've seen those items over and over again in an organized way making it easy for you to memorize the store. You can categorize 30,000 items in one location.

Grammar in 19th century dictionaries is defined as the science of vocabulary.

You also have memorized great detail about every item. You know which are fresh and which are processed. You can read the ingredients labels on items you purchase regularly and make choices based on quality and price. You can go home and taste the item, determine if you like the taste, and then remember that information when you go to purchase the product again. You learn which butchers point you to the best meat and which produce managers will get the latest shipment of fruit from the back refrigerator for you. You learn the store's marketing system and discover the best times to shop for the best prices. You manage whole fields of information associated with thousands of items in just one of the very many stores you visit each week. You are a genius!

Well, I propose a good education teaches a child how to build a grocery store of the mind for every subject. You not only feed children information to put on the shelves of the mind but help the student see ways to organize the information for quick retrieval. So when the mind searches for an idea or fact, you have a place where the mind's eye goes to either retrieve currently stored related facts or "shelve" new facts. If your grocery store started carrying organic eggs, they would have to decide whether they would put them in a new organic section, or with the current eggs, or maybe in a new temporary, promotional location in the front of the store until customers knew it was regularly available to buy. We need to teach our children to do the same thing with new facts. Are there multiple ways to pronounce a word? Is there more than one way to write a mathematical formula? Do I file a fact in just one place because I'm new at this grammar and I need to retrieve it easily until I understand it? Or can I file it in multiple brain locations?

> *Every subject is like learning a foreign language until you have a basic grasp of vocabulary and the main ideas associated with the topic.*

So, to build the brain's knowledge store, you have to begin memorizing systems. You do that by visiting the "store of words" for any particular subject many times in an organized manner. For a student, it means repeating data (revisiting the store) in an orderly fashion (filling the shelves). So we instruct students to repeatedly draw the same continental maps as we build the geography aisle. Then eventually each continent has a shelf. We repeatedly chant the same multiplication and addition tables and laws of math as we build our math aisle. Eventually we can pull down the identity law off its shelf to use in the "balance the equation" recipe. We repeatedly list the same history timeline as we build our history aisle. Eventually, we can pull down the items "Hitler", "Napoleon" and "Alexander" to mix into our analysis of despotic rulers. We work consistently for a long time until the hard is easy. Whenever we add a new ingredient to the shelf, there is a place for it to logically live.

When the organizational system is mastered, which means quickly accessible and confidently retrieved, the information becomes very useful and can be dialectically synthesized into any new idea. So the first step is rote memorization like children have always had to do. Remember that every child learns to speak from infancy through repetition and memorization and orderly associations.

When I say memorize information, I mean it in the truest sense of the word. You have that information at your fingertips always, like the Alphabet Song, or The Pledge of Allegiance or The Lord's Prayer. I am not talking about something recited for a season and then forgotten. That's why we are building an organized storage system with key ideas forming the aisles and shelves. Some facts may fade and ebb, but we work on just enough information to provide a framework of shelves that never disappears.

Education through Dialectic

"We are living in a time when sensitivities are at the surface, often vented with cutting words. Philosophically, you can believe anything, so long as you do not claim it to be true. Morally, you can practice anything, so long as you do not claim that it is a 'better' way. Religiously, you can hold to anything,

*so long as you do not bring Jesus Christ into it.
If a spiritual idea is eastern, it is granted critical
immunity; if western, it is thoroughly criticized."*
—Ravi Zacharias, *Jesus Among Other Gods*

The dialectic stage of learning is often referred to as logic or critical thinking skills. I prefer to think of it as a dialogue to clear reasoning. The easiest way to explain the dialectic is to use examples. For instance, when I'm teaching Latin, I use the grammar rules the students have already learned in English to help them figure out the rules of Latin on their own.

I may write the words "who" and "whom" on the board, and tell the students that "who" is the subject noun (also called nominative) and that "whom" is the direct object noun (also called accusative). If we add an "m", we change the word from subject noun to direct object noun. Then I'd write the Latin words "elephantus" and "elephantum" on the board and ask the students to tell me which Latin word for elephant is the direct object. I may say, "If we add an 'm' to 'who' in order to make 'whom' the direct object, what do you think might be a clue for the Latin direct object?" Of course, elephantum is the direct object. So we can establish a preliminary rule that adding an "m" indicates the word is a direct object.

More Latin examples, like "gladius" and "gladium" may confirm the new rule. Eventually, we don't have to think so hard because we recognize that every time we see a noun end with an 'm' in Latin, it is probably a direct object. We are now able to process the grammar, understand the rule, use the facts. We are thinking dialectically. The

> *The dialectic stage of learning is often referred to as logic or critical thinking skills. I prefer to think of it as a dialogue to clear reasoning.*

dialectic skills are easier to teach if the student has a firm base of grammar — rules and vocabulary — to associate with new ideas.

Here's a dialectic process needed to score high on the SAT. Please take the time to think through the problem and notice how you use math facts you know and use them to teach yourself what you don't know.

If I tell you these formulas:
3x3=9 2x2=4 and 9+4=13 is the same as 3@2=13
4x4=16 5x5=25 and 16+25=41 is equal to 4@5=41
Could you tell me the answer to 3@5?

In other words can you take the two examples of a rule and apply it to a new problem? Can you compare what you already know with a new definition and gain new understanding?

You should get 3x3=9 and 5x5=25 and 9+25=34, so 3@5=34.

In order to define the new rule of "@", we had to use our addition, multiplication, and equality definitions from our math shelf, sequentially and logically think through the example, while holding previously learned definitions in our head, and then apply them to a new symbol. In the process, we developed an understanding for the definition of "@".

Dialectic skills are best practiced with puzzles, discussions, and group interaction led by an enthusiastic teacher. Dialectic skills are academically formalized through debate, algebra, and experiments.

So when, I say "dialectic" I think about "dialoging" with a student. A live person is needed, not a machine or book. This is the step of education where large classes and computers are ineffective. This is where we need to copy Jesus' model of discipling a few students at a time to be effective. It requires a teacher to help the student appropriately question information, hold together many ideas, and develop logical conclusions.

Education through Rhetoric

"Rhetoric may be defined as the faculty of observing in any given case the available means of persuasion."
—Aristotle, *Rhetoric*, Chapter Two

Rhetoric is a well designed course of study formalized by Aristotle and usually taught as a course in classical universities and some high schools. Rhetoric has come to mean "sound bite" and propaganda to moderns. To classical, Christian students, it means to practice very specific skills in order to be the most persuasive in expressing truth, goodness, and beauty.

Rhetorical skills are the final tools needed that give students the ability to study and learn anything they set their minds to. Almost any skilled person you encounter must have these tools to be successful in his/her field.

For example, a good car mechanic is usually a great rhetorician. First, he learned his grammar. He knows the names of all the parts of the car engine. He knows the vocabulary of his field of expertise. He learned this by spending a lot of time around cars and car magazines and car people and maybe even auto-mechanic school. He isn't trusted if he can't explain the purpose of a carburetor and a cylinder. Second, he learned to process the facts he knows about car engines. He learned how the parts of the

> *To classical, Christian students, rhetoric means to practice very specific skills in order to be the most persuasive in expressing truth, goodness, and beauty.*

car worked together. He can diagnose why one part of the car is making another work improperly. He learned this by spending a lot of time around cars and car magazines and car people and maybe even auto-mechanic school. He isn't trusted if he has to make multiple repairs before figuring out what is wrong with a vehicle. Lastly, he learned how to use his knowledge wisely. He knows how to explain to non-mechanical people what is wrong with their car, make a correct diagnosis, and even train others to know what he knows. He is a rhetorician in the field of mechanics when he can persuade others to repeatedly give him money to repair their cars and when customers even tell other people to use his services.

You can repeat the entire paragraph above by substituting the word 'surgeon' for 'car mechanic' and the idea of body parts for car parts. We have trouble trusting a surgeon with a bad beside manner. Trust comes from more than knowledge; we need to know how to wisely share that knowledge in order for us to be useful to the greater community.

A good historian goes through the same process. She learns history grammar such as a basic timeline of events to give her a mental framework on which to set new information. She learns basic geography so she can figure out where events happened. Then she learns how to process this information. Why did Robert E. Lee choose to join Jefferson Davis instead of Abraham Lincoln? What events in Lee's life made him take such an unusual stand? Geography, faith, and politics were major factors for Mr. Lee. The historian can logically analyze the facts (the grammar of her subject) and form coherent conclusions.

How come we expect athletes and musical performers to practice boring things over and over until they can make the difficult seem effortless, yet we don't expect the same from our children in math, reading, and writing? Why do we think education should be natural, experiential, and fun? We should expect all students of reading, writing, and arithmetic to strive for the same disciplined lifestyle of a great musician or professional athlete.

Recovering the classical tools of learning allows each of us to tackle new disciplines, even difficult subjects.

C.S. Lewis declared that we teach our students far too many subjects far too poorly. Yet modern parents think it is normal to have their children survey six subjects a year, while mastering none of them. I think it is better to teach your children to read, write, and cipher well in every subject and then allow your children to build upon these basic skills. Excellence requires perseverance, sweat, wrestling, time, tears, and just plain labor. If you teach yourself the skills of grammar, dialectic, and rhetoric, and then pass them onto your children, even difficult subjects become accessible for your entire family. Recovering the classical tools of learning allows each of us to tackle new disciplines, even difficult subjects. That's when the tools of learning become practical and personally empowering.

Chapter Five

The Student: Learning for Life

"But I am not here to consider the feelings of academic bodies: I am concerned only with the proper training of the mind to encounter and deal with the formidable mass of undigested problems presented to it by the modern world. For the tools of learning are the same, in any and every subject; and the person who knows how to use them will, at any age, get the mastery of a new subject in half the time and with a quarter of the effort expended by the person who has not the tools at his command."
—Dorothy Sayers, *The Lost Tools of Learning,* 1947

U sing the term "classical" education implies there are other forms of education. While there are differing approaches to education, real learning implies a student knows how to gather facts (grammar), assess and analyze information (dialectic), and then has the ability to pass that knowledge onto others (rhetoric). The classical model contains the nuts and bolts of learning, regardless of the added layers that other approaches profess. Therefore, the classical model really should be called true education. To educate means to teach a person to input knowledge, process knowledge, and use knowledge. Our senses bring information in; our brains store, sort, retrieve, and analyze information; our communication skills then allow us to share information with others. Our goal as educators is to define the basic skills that measure a person as truly educated — indicated by their ability to enthusiastically tackle new ideas, to curiously ask pointed questions, and to wisely weigh consequences before taking action.

I am interested in raising human beings that delight in the laws of God, His creation, and His creatures. When Robert and John were about to enter high school, I began to understand that if I wanted them educated well, I would have to change the way I thought about teaching. I began looking for books that described educational expectations from America's age of literacy. It took me a while to understand the different view on education they presented. I recommend that you read *Carry On, Mr. Bowditch* by Jean Lee Latham. This true story illustrates well the expectations and results of a young student who knows the tools for learning.

Parents and teachers often ask for a complete subject scope and sequence for implementing the classical model. That question reveals a lack of understanding about the classical model. Instead, here is a simple scope and sequence of the skills taught in a classical education. The focus is on goals that develop a free, competent human, able to confidently confront and conquer new ideas. The chart below lists the basic goals of a parent trying to direct a good education:

Infant to 4 years of age	4 to 8 years of age
✓ should be trained to obey their parents	✓ should be trained to clean a house
✓ should memorize songs and stories	✓ should be taught to read phonetically
✓ should learn to be kind	✓ should develop the daily habit of studying math

9 to 12 years of age	13 to 14 years of age
✔ should be trained to manage a household	✔ should be trained in vocational skills
✔ should be trained to memorize lots of facts	✔ should be taught to write well-constructed paragraphs
✔ should be taught spelling and grammar rules of languages	✔ should be taught to write well-constructed essays
✔ should be taught to write well-constructed sentences	✔ should be taught to defend ideas
✔ should be taught to write well-constructed paragraphs	✔ should be taught public speaking
	✔ should be taught formal logic
	✔ should be taught research skills

15 to 18 years of age

✔ should be taught leadership
✔ should be taught to write comparative analysis of ideas
✔ should be taught to challenge ideas

Notice that there is no mention of history or science or subjects. Classical education is different from modern education. The classical model is skill-based, not merely subject-focused. Through the acquisition of grammar, the mental gymnastics of logical processes, and the art of communication, science students learn how to:

1. memorize, sort, and retrieve scientific facts
2. read science books (there is a specific way)
3. write about science (there are expected forms)
4. enter the Great Classical Conversations about the philosophies of science

5. manage technologies while studying of creation
6. think about science, any science.

We are very blessed that we can "classically" study the "classics". In other words, we want to use the best content possible, the Western classics, to teach the classical skills of learning. So we practice acquiring grammatical, dialectic, and rhetorical skills by studying good literature, accurate science, amazing heroes, and influential philosophers, Life-learners are happy when they can read a biology text,

People often confuse memorization with "cramming." demonstrate a dissection, and write a research paper on anything from an organ's functions to the ethics of harvesting that organ. We like knowing we can be useful to others and that the joy of learning is our personal reward.

I am excited by the many families we have worked with that have successfully guided their children to a passion for life. And I see frustrated parents who have over-estimated their high school child's elementary education, realize they haven't prepared their child adequately at the grammar stage, and so lower their standards for their older child's education just at the time the student is really ready to become a mature learner.

Developmentally, young children can memorize far more easily than older children, so we talk about "grammar school" for the same ages we talk about "elementary school". We require a lot of memory work from little children because they all have brains wired to memorize. When I hear a mother say their child can't memorize, I just listen and try to figure out what she really means, as I know it is never true. They may not be fast at it or like it, but they certainly can memorize, otherwise they couldn't speak. How did your child learn to talk? They heard you say "mommy" a thousand times until they could use it correctly. Isn't that memorization? Once I can say, "The stove is hot." with understanding, I can use those four words forever. People confuse memorization with "cramming". In the classical model, memorizing grammar implies hearing, seeing, and using new vocabulary until it finds a comfortable location on the proper shelf in the normal bank of words or ideas that you pull from.

Even though this is how God designed infants to learn, adults have to do the same thing when encountering a new subject. You can be 4 or 44 years old and still be a grammarian. All subjects seem like foreign languages until you know their grammar. That's why the first tool of learning is the art of mastering the vocabulary of a subject. More mature brains tend to link vocabulary with understanding sooner. Little children are more content with memorizing a song about the kings of England without caring who each king was or why he became king. They just want to sing the fun song or say the silly chant. If they ask "Why?", then answer them.

Teachers lose a lot of time waiting for understanding to occur before they teach something new. I don't care if my sons understand the periodic table of chemistry in 3rd grade, but I know it is easiest to memorize in elementary school. They won't want to memorize it in middle school like they do in their younger years. But when they get to high school, all the preparation will pay off.

As our older boys got older, it became important to look outward and teach our boys to be useful to the larger community. We were blessed with a very active youth ministry in our church, so they were already involved in local missions. Both boys are athletic, so we spent 15 years learning the politics of children's sports. Since working in the community was a priority, we found wonderful men who gave great employment opportunities to our boys. During this time, I realized I also wanted to improve the academic education that we were giving our boys and share our experiences with interested families.

I was saddened as more of my home schooling friends began putting their children in full-time, peer-based, institutional education due to the fear of teaching high school subjects. This was in the 1990's before every family had a computer let alone access to the Internet. Also, no one was around to advise parents about home schooling through high school, so the concerns of these parents were understandable. Rob and I liked being with our children, and we were not fearful of our own academic inadequacies. Our eldest son, Robert, was finally old enough to do what was important to him, and I knew we would work hard to help him achieve his dreams. But, I recognized the seriousness of academics in preparation for college and so, Rob and I looked at schooling options.

> *The Great Classical Conversations represent the main streams of foundational ideas that humans have debated throughout history as we contemplate God's purposes and our response.*

We visited high schools, talked to head masters, and looked around for a classical model of education. It just didn't exist in our area at that time. I've come to realize it still doesn't exist very often. Classical education is such a hard concept for modern minds to grasp, that well-meaning, classical school headmasters often end up succumbing to parental demands for modern school texts and methods. Also, classical schools often have a difficult time finding teachers who can actually teach classically.

In the end, Rob advised that we have a few students come to our home and join us for our own classical program. In this way, I could help with the subjects that made my friends wary like Algebra II and Chemistry and Foreign

Language, Robert could work with a small peer group that would enable him to work on rhetorical skills like debate and presentations, and I wouldn't have to run him all over the place for classes like I was already doing for his sports. We had eleven students join us for six subjects that fall and ended up with six students in the winter semester that could actually complete the work I assigned. Notice I said "subjects." I was just beginning to make the transition from content to skills and hadn't begun to think classically. It takes a long time to break old thought habits.

I was earning a little bit of money and having a blast guiding these very smart students through some very challenging material. More families asked if they could join my program. So I hired some experienced home schooling friends to help and began Classical Conversations to help other families enjoy a classical education from home. Our adventure in helping others participate in Home-Centered Education continues to grow and I hope to be helpful to more families.

Success Stories — Robert and Nate

Here's how Home-Centered Education looked for our eldest son in high school. Robert participated in Classical Conversations once a week with his assignments completed so he could make presentations, share projects, and team up for debates and labs with other like-minded students. He worked a full day a week with a technology firm as an engineering aid. He played basketball all over the east coast with AAU, Jr. Hornets, private school teams, recreational leagues, and our county's home school league. Robert was part of a vibrant youth group at church and was able to go on many mission trips both at home and abroad. He also took a few state university courses to provide additional preparation for college. So even though Robert was home schooled until he was 17 and left for college, he was certainly not at home very much.

Robert had a successful Home-Centered Education that enabled him to attend a very selective university, Clemson, and have Ethicon, a Johnson & Johnson company, pay for most of his college by working for them as a co-op student. After spending seven years watching him chase a basketball around courts all over the country, Robert stunned us all by choosing to play collegiate rugby. He had never played rugby before in his life, but he knew how to learn anything well. Incredibly, he was named Clemson Rugby Rookie of the Year and went on to become nationally ranked in the sport while working part time and studying engineering. Rugby is both a club sport and a collegiate sport. This enabled Robert to play in multiple countries as well as all over the United States. He met men and made relationships that have lasted past graduation. Robert was hired in 2006 as an industrial engineer in the manager trainee program with UPS. He took the position, as it was an impressive addition to his resume. After a year, he moved upward with a smaller technical firm and has begun purchasing a number of investment properties.

I'm equally proud of Nate, Robert's best friend. He also participated in Classical Conversations. Besides working hard at academics, he was hired to be a lab tech at Wake Forest University. At sixteen years old, he was preparing standard slides for researchers to use to compare to patients' lab work. He learned how to operate one of the most expensive electron microscopes in the world, a machine that graduate students are rarely allowed to use. He also worked summers with a German company here in the US in a lab that manufactures DNA.

His SAT scores and high school employment helped him to receive a full scholarship to a small private college known for its excellent biology department, and Nate is now continuing his education at a state school where he wants to become a biology teacher. In high school, Nate took a few community college courses. He was also very active in mission work and sports and pursued his passion for music. Nate reads a lot and enjoys engaging thoughtful participants in the Great Classical Conversations. He has traveled a lot, and he loves playing music for friends and family. Nate, too, had parents who directed his education while challenging him to find mentors wherever he went.

More Success Stories — Emily, Kristen, and Jen

I'd also like to tell you about Emily, the first graduate from Classical Conversations. She was more of a home body then the other two and focused her time on creating her own high school curriculum. She pursued music, debate, politics, and mission work during high school. She went to undergraduate school at Campbell University, earned her masters and went to Oxford all on scholarship. She spent summers working at the Pentagon and now works for the FBI as an analyst. I tease her that she is a "Bond Girl", and I am proud to know that she is one of the many great citizens protecting our country.

I love telling families about Kristen and Jen, two sisters from our support group. Both left Classical Conversations with a lot of college work already completed through Advanced Placement, SAT II subject tests, and Wake Forest University dual-enrollment classes. They both attended universities on scholarships. Both traveled extensively in high school, worked jobs, and pursued personal passions. They have both studied abroad at different colleges in foreign countries. Kristin began working as a physics research assistant after her freshmen year and studied many languages. She worked with the international science community presenting at symposiums before finishing college. She chooses now to use her love of learning and languages in the mission field. I am proud that she is a scientist and linguist who is using her talents for eternity's sake. Jen continues her writing and literature studies while practicing ballroom dancing and publishing study guides. She too has enjoyed learning many languages and traveling around the world. Her love of life is reflected in the care she uses as she chooses words for her books.

These students didn't go to college and just have all these marvelous opportunities present themselves. They had parents who directed a lot of excellent opportunities in high school that prepared them for the world. Their parents couldn't have kept them home in a building if they wanted to. The world was their classroom. Their parents prepared themselves to teach their young children well, and the love of life and learning was caught by their children as they saw their parents attend educational conferences, take academic courses, and teach Sunday School. These parents modeled the delight of learning with their children to the extent that they thought it was normal to work through a math text or science book or English grammar as a family.

> *These parents modeled the delight of learning with their children to the extent that they thought it was normal to work through a math text or science book or English grammar as a family.*

None of the families mentioned have a lot of money. All of them live on one income and have an average of 3.5 children. But every one of these parents is dedicated to being the main mentor for their children as they help their student facilitate the choices of a true education. They find as many challenging opportunities for learning as they possibly can while still preparing their students for the rigorous academics tested in Advanced Placement tests and SAT II subject tests.

For these parents, Home-Centered Education meant a lot of time spent with little ones evolving into a lot of highly academic and vocational time spent with the older children. Teaching reading is best done with a child on someone's lap. Teaching math is best done sitting near a student as they work through a text. Teaching writing is best done through sharing the joy of words on paper. As their children grew physically, these families found social, academic, athletic, and vocational opportunities in an ever-lengthening radius from home. The success of these families and students should encourage us in considering the validity of the success of Home-Centered Education, which truly prepares a student for a life of learning.

❧ Challenged to be Ready ❧
by Luke Morales

When I first began a course of classes called Classical Conversations, I was skeptical of the whole thing and a bit apprehensive with the name "Challenge A". But I soon discovered my criticisms to be unfounded. Every class and session held something new; each dialogue between student and teacher, each conversation or debate, began to mold in me the skills that would be needed in my pre-college years.

In Challenge A, I was taught how to formulate a bibliography; in Challenge B, how to take "copious notes" (as tutor Mrs. Tomkinson called it). Challenge I brought on a wave of philosophical and theological debates, whereas Challenge II required that I articulate my opinions and portray my views in a persuasive manner.

And what have I just described? Were all these classes meant to directly impose the stand point of a college prep course? Perhaps — for in all things we are constantly being shaped into the people that we will become. But, (unbeknownst to me) in my attempts to finish homework and beat the deadlines of these classes, I was being shown the exact things that I would soon be facing in the coming years.

As I began to apply to the colleges of my choice, including the process of writing essays for application, I found that the skills (and the endurance) needed had already been molded into my character. Now — don't get me wrong — this is not a vague attempt to blow my own horn. It is instead praise, a tribute to those who taught and invested and loved me though my high school years.

As I wrote an essay entitled "What is your academic passion?" I began as I had always been instructed: Start with an outline: the introduction, the body, the conclusion. And a "dreaded" college essay was finished — made into just another assignment, a deadline, or another paper of 500 words (a very common task in Classical Conversations).

While sitting in an English class of college level metaphysical poetry, I saw that I had already acquired the thought processes needed to comprehend this information — honed into my character by the years of classes. The same endurance taught in Challenge I, the same patience learned, all were the exact skills that I was now using in the college classroom.

When asking a professor what was most needed to complete a major in English, I was amused (and startled) by his response: "A basic knowledge of English grammar; the paragraph and sentence structure; verb tenses and such — many who begin as English majors don't realize that these things are needed." I sat there, remembering with a quiet appreciation all the times my grammar had been corrected, every hard (but needed) critique, and every instant when I was pushed to do my best in every aptly-named Challenge class. Each lesson learned and each invaluable minute spent in these classes has molded and changed me, down to the way in which I look at my life and the way I see my God. Through these experiences, and through these classes, I have truly been blessed. ✖

Chapter Six

The Parent: Committing To Basic Principles

"The ability to learn on one's own is normally a result of good education, and not normally the cause of it."
—Doug Wilson, *Classical Education & the Home School*

Changes in the 21st century are forcing parents to think from a new perspective about what makes a good education. I contend that it involves a truly Home-Centered Education, and I want to encourage you to consider three guiding principles.

Principle #1: I am going to work hard and consistently as my child's primary discipler.

Ground your children in reality while presenting the impossible as possible. I have two very negative children who shoot down every idea I have. And I have two whose thoughts soar when I give them a new idea. Yet, I pester them all with new ideas because every now and then even the pessimists' eyes light up and they begin to ask questions. My children complain everyday about something being too hard or not fun and every day my husband and I reply with things like, "try being enslaved to a job when you're grown." or, "try doing this as an orphan, or as a hungry child in Africa." My husband talks to them about responsibility and I talk to them about possibilities. We remind them that we just want the best for them and that one day they may want to make a blockbuster movie, or save a dying child, or create a lot of high paying jobs for their community. They don't know what the world holds for them and what the Lord will expect from them, so they need to be ready to do all things through Christ who strengthens them. We read a lot of books and tell a lot of stories about children who have joy amid hardships because otherwise all my boys will experience are the stories of the wealthy American kids they hang around. I recommend reading *The Little Britches* series, *Carry On, Mr. Bowditch*, *The Great Brain* series, and *The Little House on the Prairie* series for true stories about American children. I also recommend most Newbery Literature for fiction set in historical events. Even though we use technology, books are our priority because you can't cuddle up with a laptop, at least not yet. Also, the Internet can never disciple a child. That takes lots of time with a warm body.

Make reading a priority in your home

We happen to know our family's history and parts of it were very hard, so we share stories about their grandparents with our boys. Telling good stories provides the seeds for building trust and joy as your child's teacher. We read and discuss the Bible most days and are always talking about current events. My kids love hearing *The Story of The World* series from Peace Hill Press in the car, but they will quickly turn it off if I'm in the mood to discuss current events like the wars in Asia or the economic struggles of Africa. They are children and they want to hear facts and have them explained through stories. Parents tell me all the time that they don't know these kinds of stories, so where do you begin. Well you just begin…

Start by reading aloud daily with your family. I mean an hour a day or more. They read to you, you read to them, and you all read silently. Give away the TV and video games and magazine subscriptions if the screens in your life are stopping you from choosing the best activities with your family. This is hard to do. You don't want to. Okay, then figure out a way to keep them and spend a lot of time reading with your kids. I grappled with this issue for about three years with my older boys. I finally gave the TV away. Then, there was nothing to do at night but read and play games together. Now, we have a TV and video games, but we must struggle to keep them from ruling our lives.

"We have to deal with retraining our children as well as ourselves to not love the very technologies that undo our capacities to think (and our capacities to disciple)…"

Controlling technology is hardest on Mom and Dad, as video screens provide much free time for us. We have to deal with retraining our children as well as ourselves to not love the very technologies that undo our capacities to think, (and our capacities to disciple) as Neil Postman warned in *Amusing Ourselves to Death*. Stories and conversations related by real people can reach deep into souls. So begin equipping yourself for the fun part of the hard work by reading a lot. Now you may say, "I'm not a reader, but I am a listener and thinker." You owe it to your children to become a reader. Most modern adults who aren't readers were never given good advice or the time to become a good reader. You will find that the more picture books and children's novels you read aloud to your children, the quicker you will become at reading, while expanding your personal enjoyment. Just the pleasure of the close relationship developed as you cuddle together will encourage your whole family to read more.

Home-Centered Education requires consistency. My friend, Jayne, gave this illustration of true consistency. Jayne has two boys with severe learning issues and is fortunate to have enough love for her boys to fight with them and for them in finding the best teachers and methods of instruction. She and her husband make their home the base of learning. She pays for some professional help for the children, but more importantly, she pays for help to train herself. It costs less in time and money to send yourself to an expert and then use that knowledge to help all of your children. Instead, most of us send our individual students to experts and never even see what the professional is doing. We need to educate ourselves on how to be able to reinforce the expert's advice at home.

Jayne's epiphany came from her grandmother and milking the cow. On the day her grandmother died the cow got milked. On the day all the relatives came for the funeral, the cow got milked. No matter what happened the cow got milked. Are our children somehow of less value than a cow? Where did this idea come from that learning should be seasonal and only 180 days a year? I know you'll respond that it came from our agricultural heritage, but that's only half the story. When farm kids weren't at school they were learning to work to eat. They were pursuing the love of life and learning with their mother, father, or neighbors. They didn't stay home to vacation or play games. They were being educated with life skills. The parent determined when they would do book learning and

> *Home-Centered Education requires consistency.*

when they would do life learning, but the family worked very hard at both all year round.

So, the first step to success is to act consistently. Everyday we read. Everyday we work math problems. Everyday we learn how to lead a family. Everyday we learn how to rise above our natural tendencies. By acting this way through a few formative years, the pattern is established and our children become part of the team rather than a force that saps our parental strength. Our teens were fun to be with and liked their family just as they did as youngsters. But again, it's the parents' attitude that makes this happen. If you don't want to milk the cow, don't be surprised at loud moaning and raucous behavior coming from the barn.

Does this level of consistency sound difficult? It is. But consider the alternatives. Consistency is what allows humans to write great books, develop new technologies, become life-saving surgeons, send projects into space, or become the next Michael Jordon. Life-time learners know when the work is done the fun is begun. Are you only content with a child that can get a good job? Or are you beginning to want to do the hard work it takes to love your child into greatness? I suggest you begin by learning to love telling stories and consistently expect some academics to be completed everyday.

The next step is to be very clear about your child's abilities. Teachers and parents tend to overestimate children's experience and underestimate children's abilities. Mothers tell their kids to clean up their room everyday only to be disappointed when the child declares the room is clean. This is because children don't have an adult's experience. Adults know how to make a bed without wrinkles. It occurs to you to check behind the drapes for dirty socks. You know how to hang clothes straight and on the right type of hangers. Children have the ability to do all of the above, but they don't have the experience to do it on their own. An adult or older child must show them many, many times how to make the bed with the corners tucked in. They must be given lots of practice in buttoning collars in order to hang their dress clothes up properly.

One of the reasons we become frustrated is because we forget they are children and we are adults. We actually can retain and process information more quickly than they. Have you ever been in a situation where you asked your child to relate some academic information to someone else and they couldn't? You remember studying the information and were really pleased with the progress they made in their lesson. Then a few days or months later, you remember it and they don't. The information went in and out of their head. They have the ability to learn the information. They don't have the experience required to dialectically process the information away from the context of a lesson as quickly as their teacher. So the teacher thinks the student knows something that he or she really has only surveyed or been introduced to. Just like making a bed, children need to be shown the same academic material repeatedly before being able to process it readily and easily.

Once, I was leading a class in a lesson we had been working on for 14 weeks. In the middle of the lesson, a fifth grader blurted out, "I actually understand what I am doing!" He had been co-operative and completed similar assignments during the previous 14 weeks, but he was just mimicking me, his teacher. Now, he is able to take all that practice and actually think it through to use it in new ways. A single light bulb turned on. But I have to remember as his teacher that he still needs lots of practice in similar examples to ensure he doesn't forget what he has learned. Eventually, he will be able to use his new processing skill in things he is teaching himself. The dialectic process — the ability to use, understand and analyze the things we know is built through drilling facts and analyzing them in context.

Another time, a darling little boy announced to his class during a history lesson that his cousin was Virginia Dare. The moms all looked at each other, trying to process what that could mean. Wasn't she lost in Roanoke when the English returned and found the village decimated? Did she make it somehow? Or do we have our facts confused? Is his cousin named Virginia Dare by coincidence? He's eight years old and is repeating a fact jogged from his memory. The ability for it to be true isn't important to him. It's just like my eight year old son thinking he is a great snow skier. He's often a legend in his own mind because he lacks the experience and perspective to judge accurately. Yet, he has the ability to be taught to be a great snow skier for his age, if he is given the chance to practice.

The confusion between ability and enough experience to use a skill or information becomes apparent when students are in high school. I constantly have parents of elementary age children tell me, "My child is great at arithmetic so I let them skip every other problem in the math book." Invariably, the same day, another mother will call me to say, "Why is algebra so hard? My child hates it. We're just going to get through geometry and take consumer math. I guess she just isn't a math person..." When you dig into the student's preparation you often find out that math was easy for them when they were younger but no one insisted on the rigorous practice which would enable the subject to remain easy as the concepts became more difficult. Or, a parent of a middle school student will call and ask, "My child really knows English grammar, so can he just take the writing portion of your workshop and skip the grammar?" Then I'll get a call from a high school mother wanting a Latin or Spanish tutor to keep their child from failing a course. "I just need to get them through this credit so I can get them into a state university." They should have been drilled in English grammar so they could understand the foreign language. Now that they are almost finished with high school, no one cares if they actually learn something. They just need to get the credit. Of course they can't learn algebra or French because they weren't taught how to teach themselves the basic grammar of their subject. Americans have a very high self image of their intellectual abilities while actually knowing very little. Every other country in the world has a lower estimation of their academic abilities and yet, they are measurably more educated than we are.

So we need to be very honest about our child's abilities. If your child has always lived in America, they do not know enough English grammar and basic math facts. Want proof? Go ask them to explain how they distinguish the difference between an object complement and a direct object. Or ask "What is the first person plural imperfect past tense of the verb 'To Be?'" If they can't answer these basic questions in English, they'll struggle with learning foreign languages. Or ask them the factors of some common number like 52 or 121. I have had many adults who are editors tell me they had Latin in school and never use it. Almost all adult Americans know only spoken English and they get along just fine. So why do I keep insisting these skills are important? In this age of globalism, only knowing spoken English will cease to be adequate for our next generation to earn a living, let alone be world leaders.

Principle #2: I am going to concentrate on teaching my student the tools of learning anything.

I recently watched a well-respected public school teacher prepare 40 students ages 7 to 12 for a state-wide orchestra performance. She's a good teacher because she's chosen material that appeals to all ages and she makes them practice it until they are proud of themselves and the hard work they put into it. How dare she ask my child to stand in front of hundreds of people without making them work hard! I would be disappointed for my children if the performance was poor and I would be frustrated at the time misspent. Instead, after only two practices I'm crying tears of pride at the skill these children exhibit. She is a very good music teacher.

The key to a classical education is modeling. Nothing is expected of the student but to repeat the same thing a million times in a million ways until they are capable of always using that skill or information in any setting and in a way that commands the respect of others. Every band or orchestra teacher must use good teaching skills in order to keep the attention of students with a variety of ages and skill levels and different instruments and different parts of a composition while moving them towards the mastery of a piece of complex music performed in a way that impresses their audience. These are the same skills required of a good classroom teacher, yet we never clearly define for the students or teacher exactly what the end result should be. Orchestra members can hear a recording and know how they should finally sound. Does a math teacher ever get to have a mathematician perform for her students so they know what to expect? Does a history teacher ever get to say, "You have completed this course when you can recite these 200 historic events in order," and then demonstrate the recitation of the timeline for the student? Does a chemistry teacher get to define a handful of experiments that the students perform over and over until they get the same data she gets at the same precision she demands? Most students don't really know what they are to master, why they are to master it, or are given the skills to master the information. Therefore we must define the information and model the process for them.

I am studying for my Doctorate in Ministry in Global Church-Based Education. I have never done that before. I don't really know what will make my professors give me an "A". I barely know who they are, let alone how their minds work. I have never written a many hundred page thesis before. I've written short research papers. I've written long books. But, I have never had to combine them before. For me, it is much harder to write a very long, professional paper. I have done as much as I know to do on my own. Now I have to study a variety of published theses and figure out what to do next. I have to copy the experts. I'll ask my professors questions. I'll talk to my classmates. I'll have to struggle for a while until I find my own voice within this new task. I don't like how I feel about this. It is work, but I have to do it. I know I can do this because I know how to learn. So, I am not afraid, and I'm even excited about the results, whether I get an "A" or not. I know I'll be able to do something I've never done before. I have to psych myself up as much as I did the first time I went to jump off a twelve foot cliff into an underwater cenote (limestone pit) full of 150 feet of very dark water. I screamed all the way down, but I sure loved yelling, "I did it!" when I surfaced. When I made another visit to the cenote, I jumped many times. It was easy after the first time. A major block to learning is the fear of doing something new.

The key to a classical education is modeling.

Academic goals for inexperienced students should be clearly defined tasks, starting with mastering basic skills. As the student matures, they need to read, research, record, and refine information concerning a myriad of topics. These skills require a lifetime of practice to do well. So older students may be encouraged to survey a lot of content while practicing specific research and writing skills. They need to research important, relevant material, but the focus is on research skills, presentation skills, analytical thinking, comparative analysis, and writing, writing, writing. As they progress in the aforementioned skills, they need to add discussion, debate, and presentation skills. The interesting thing about these skills is that they are much more interesting to the student if they know how to organize and retrieve data. All the early grammar preparation through memorization will pay off in middle school and high school as they dig more deeply into topics. A common concern parents have in a classical high school is the sense that the students move through too much material too quickly, especially if their child didn't have a good grammatical foundation. Their children are not used to being confronted with a large amount of information and then sorting it for the key ideas and important concepts. They don't know how to make an outline in their minds to build from, and they aren't used to storing large quantities of ideas in an organized manner. The students don't know how to use the book well, so we reduce the information required for them to study, instead of teaching them how to break big ideas down into manageable steps.

We recently enjoyed the fruits of many years of art history studies with our young children when a friend of mine invited us to attend a large art museum. We left after five hours. Art lovers probably dream of five hours in a museum, but would you expect to be able to do that with five children 8-13 years old? We enjoyed every minute, because our children had already spent time regularly studying art history and color composition. They recognized Dutch renaissance art and how its rich colors differed from the gold and temperas used by Giotto. They understood Monet's influence on the art world because they had painted pictures modeling his techniques. They knew that the Minoan culture differed from the Mycenaean culture and were curious about the differences in their statues. The grammar made the hands-on experience meaningful. As we continue in our art history studies, the museum trip will allow them to say, "I saw that" and make even more connections between the art they saw, the science needed to create the art, and the history behind the pieces. They will be able to talk to artists, curators, and grandparents about why they enjoy certain pieces of work and share that joy with others. Modern educators think going to a museum will help children like learning art history. That's backwards. Spending some intensive time studying the grammar of art will make the art museum experience more interesting. The reward for mastering art facts, a few drawing rules, and artistic techniques is the ability to enter the Great Classical Conversation about man's place throughout history and how he chooses to glorify God.

Lots of teachers and parents tell me I'm wrong to make my kids sing skip counting songs, drill math facts, and work every math problem in a text until they can solve it with speed and accuracy. But they wouldn't tell me I was wrong to make them practice musical scales over and over. And therein is the problem with modern education. Our educationally-tracked students are never shown that the skills used to study music, math, basketball, and foreign language are the same. If you can study one area well, you can use those same tools to study another area that may be more difficult or less interesting to you.

Here are some interesting myths and truths to consider along this educational journey...

Myth	Truth
School work must be fun, experiential, amusing, and applicable.	School work is hard, requires discipline, and becomes fun once the basics are mastered.

Myth	Truth
You can use a calculator or the internet to look things up.	You need a place to begin to look things up and you can't trust that your calculator is correct if you don't have a reference number in your brain. As Sheila Taylor said in Essentials when the kids cheered because she lost her teaching notes, "I may have lost my notes but I didn't lose my brain."
Students don't need to know English grammar.	English will soon be one of many languages spoken in America. TV shows based in Miami, LA, and New York already portray bilingual police officers.
My child should be taught using their learning style.	Children should be taught how to use their learning style to study difficult ideas.
My child can't do _____.	To be human means to rise above our nature. Our giftedness can be used to strengthen our weaknesses instead of neglecting them. See Helen Keller.
My student is going to be (fill in the blank) so they don't need to study this.	The average person will have multiple careers and will raise children with different interests. Education is for life and for the generations.
My child has already studied that subject.	Wow, you mean they know everything about that subject?
My child won't listen to me so he needs a different teacher.	My child won't listen to me so we both have some serious character development to work on.

Principle #3: I am going to find many resources that challenge my child's mind and heart, as well as finding like-minded companions for the journey.

Textbooks

The textbooks you use will not make as much difference in a Home-Centered Education compared to the way a student uses a textbook. This is a revolutionary thought for many, so I recommend you read James Sire's *How to Read a Book Slowly* or Mortimer Adler's *How to Read a Book*. Many books explain how to read well, but usually people who already read well are the only ones who know that different material requires different styles of reading for different goals. If you don't like to read, you may not like these books. That's why I recommended beginning with children's books and novels. I believe, like C.S. Lewis, that there is no such thing as a children's book. If there is a good story to be told, then all ages will enjoy the book. Otherwise, probably no one will like the story anyway. So, if you already enjoy reading stories, the above mentioned books will help you learn to read books that are not stories.

> *Our educationally-tracked students are never shown that the skills used to study music, math, basketball, and foreign language are the same.*

Here's a quick hint on how to prove you understand a high school text book. Take the table of contents and use it as a guide. Then write your own chapter for each chapter in the book, using the textbook as your source of information. In other words, write your own synopsis and illustrations of the key points from each chapter in a manner that others can learn from. If you can do this, you can keep the notebook and add to it as you learn more about the same subject. You will be a truly educated person.

If you are not used to learning this way, it can sound very hard. Well, clear understanding requires quality study skills. It does become much easier the longer you study this way.

Technology

Technology can bring the best of information to your home, and even great teachers through audio and video, but it is one-sided. We can yell at the annoying 'talking head' all we want on the cable news show, but he can't hear us. Learning is a two-way street. There must be someone to talk to while you are learning. You can't fully rely on technology to help your child learn, unless you actively participate with the technology, too. Suppose your child is studying geometry and the computer program worked great through the first nine Euclidean proofs. But now, they are struggling with the tenth proof. If you are unfamiliar with the first nine, it will be hard to help them when they come to you with questions on the tenth proof. So parents tend to conclude that the program is no good, or their child's not good at a subject, when really they wrongly assumed learning could be done without a mentor. Now, I haven't always been able to immediately help my students with a calculus or chemistry problem because they usually are working on a text alone at that age. But I have always paid close attention to how their text was set up so that I can help them look back to where they got lost and reread and study the difficult problem with them. I don't have to know how to solve a specific problem or read an entire piece of literature, but I do need to know how to help them sort through information and find the answer. Just talking aloud to an interested adult who's not afraid to try to help can often be enough for an engaged student to solve a problem.

The same is true for foreign language. My students may have surpassed me in vocabulary and translation, but I can know enough about their text to help them find where the answer to their question was taught. And I can always use flash cards to drill them on their vocabulary words. As the adult responsible for the child's education, you either need to be able to teach the subject, have the time to learn the subject with the student, or have enough study skills to direct a child to the location of an answer. The answer may be found in another person outside of your family, but that requires a community to inquire of, hence, the importance of support groups in Home-Centered Education.

Friends for your Children

Move heaven and earth to find a best friend who is also educated from home for your older children as they naturally grow away from their parents' instruction. Learning is a journey and it requires a good friend to share in the joy. It is okay if that best friend is mom or dad. That wasn't our family's situation, but it is in many cases. My best friend through the boys' high school years was the mother of their best friends. Our families encouraged one another throughout the high school years. My boys think it's nice to have two mothers and two fathers. They sure needed all of us when they got into trouble.

Inspirational Mentors

Find teachers or tutors for your students and recognize you are not paying for the information that person has as much as for the time spent with someone who loves learning. I have a friend without a lot of money who pays to have her son study with one of the tutors in our Home-Centered Education support group. She told a bunch of other parents one night that she'd pay for her sons to haul dirt just to be around this tutor because she knew all that he would learn just from being near her. It's no surprise that her boys are now the students other adults go out of their way to help mentor. Her teenagers are a pleasure to be around.

I feel that way about all the families I've described. They raise children that are respected. That's why it's important for me to direct the choices available for my children's education. I need to help them choose the right kind of influence to be around. And unlike the ads on TV, it's not to keep my kids off drugs; that's a given. It's to influence my boys to choose excellence. We often confuse average with normal. It is normal for a 20 year old man to run 15 miles. It is average for a 20 year old man to run one mile and be exhausted. Strive for role models who show your children what they were created to do and not just what it takes to make the grade.

Find teachers or tutors for your students and recognize you are not paying for the information that person has as much as for the time spent with someone who loves learning.

I am not the best math teacher in the world based on my knowledge of math. Someone like Einstein would be a better pick. But I love learning math, and students who spend time with me figure that out very quickly. Every math problem is a mountain to be leveled and made accessible to me. So I try to show them how to level the mountain. That means false starts, ridiculous answers, quiet moments, lots of laughing, and quantities of time spent wrestling with new concepts. I try to remove fear of the unknown and to break down academic canyons into baby steps you can climb one at a time. I take pleasure in discovering the process to a solution.

The mind behind a course is much more important than the course topic or credit earned if you are interested in being educated. Tony Campolo in his article *"Missing the Point: Seminary"* reminds us that…

"It doesn't matter what the course is — learning at the feet of a great scholar marks a student forever. If you find yourself in seminary, concern yourself not so much with what courses you take, but from whom you take them. You'll forget most subject matter within a decade, but the influence of a memorable instructor stays with you for a lifetime."[1]

I'd say this is true for any learning environment, and it bothers me that some parents still look for the name of a university rather than the name of the dean heading the student's choice of college or certain remarkable professors. This is very easy to find out now from the Internet. The dean of a department or college determines who is hired, what is taught, and through what forms of communication. You may find a world-renown expert serving as a dean in a lesser known school that will be eager to help your student find scholarships or unusual learning opportunities.

I once had a college professor that the students didn't appreciate. She taught a hard subject and there really wasn't enough time in class to teach it well. We were college students and expected to wrestle with the material, hire tutors, join study groups, and attend office hours. She was the only female professor in our aerospace engineering department at that time and that intrigued me. Also, I was at that point where I was learning to really learn, and I wanted a B desperately as I knew I could never get an A. There just wasn't time for me to learn it well enough. The prevailing class attitude was, give me a C and get me out of here. Well, I no longer had that attitude, and so I worked hard and got to know more about this woman than the outfit she wore on a stage before 40 students twice a week. Turned out she was a little odd. But then you'd have to be odd to be the first female in a man's field. But the time spent with her gave me something beyond the C I finally earned (by the skin of my teeth). She got to know me and saw something in me that she wanted to encourage. I may have only gotten a C and not my coveted B, but she inspired me not to give up in aerospace, suggested some classes I should take, found a role for me in a PBS TV documentary on women in science, and wrote employment references for me. It was the best C I ever earned! The students who studied with her were very, very smart and yet teased me because I had made friends with this unpopular teacher. The experience showed me the immaturity of most college students and the value of getting to know someone who knows what you want to know.

Why did that teacher do more for me, even though I was a C student? Why do we ignore some students and are drawn to helping others? Most of us want to be around passionate, open people. Teachers want to help students who seek knowledge, are moldable and want to go the extra yard. They like students who look at life as an adventure instead of groaning at the next task. When an adult seeks your child out, even to be hard on them, think about why. There are a lot of other people they could have chosen to become interested in, yet they chose your child to spend the time and energy on. Listen and don't be defensive. I never feel like I'm getting my money's worth if a teacher doesn't point out how my child can improve. If I was happy with the status quo in their education, I could just quit caring about it. Look for those who will challenge your child, and if your child rises to the challenge, then maybe one day your child may actually come to value their experience with that difficult tutor. It's so rewarding for me to get letters from grown students apologizing for their behavior in my class and thanking me for expecting much from them.

So, try to teach your students to respect mentors for their accomplishments and not their personalities. This is hard in the feel popular era of Brittany Spears and Tom Cruise because we teach our children to connect personality with success. Try to teach them to connect character with success. And then prove you mean it by being willing to pay for them to just haul dirt for a dedicated mentor.

As parents guiding the journey of a young child to adulthood, consider living by these guiding principles. The basic principles of consistency and modeling, teaching the tools of learning, and finding like-minded sojourners for your family and inspirational mentors for your children will serve you well as you raise children capable of learning anything.

[1] McLaren, Brian D. & Campolo, Tony 2003. *Adventures in Missing the Point: How the Culture Controlled Church Neutered the Gospel.* Zondervan/Youth Specialties.

quote, page 65:

Wilson, Douglas & Jones, Douglas & Calihan, Wes 1999. *Classical Education & The Home School.* Canon Press.

Chapter Seven

The Purpose: Studying to Glorify God

> *"By wisdom a house is built, and by understanding it is established, and by knowledge are the chambers filled with all precious and pleasant riches."*
> —Proverbs 24:3, 4

J eff Reed, a leader in developing wisdom-based learning materials for church-based education, has written a wisdom assessment tool entitled *The 7th Priority*. In it, he states,

> *"Ancient wisdom gets right at the heart of the point. It calls for every individual to become committed to the lifelong pursuit of wisdom. Without this commitment, right from the very early stages of life, it is impossible to live a skillful life."* [1]

Too many people are content to let their children pursue knowledge apart from relationship, just like Bible scholars who don't know Jesus. We need to learn how to devour facts, process them for pertinent themes and applications, and then use the knowledge gained and understood to pursue wisdom.

We should expect our eighteen-year-old youths to be equipped to lead others to wise decisions. Instead, we have generally inspired our young adults to accept low standards of literacy and a self-centeredness that precludes understanding that they can even have a global impact. Hollywood makes great movies depicting teachers that students can't help but admire. But teachers come and go from our lives. How many parents are portrayed as equipped to handle their children's homework, let alone demonstrate the joy of encouraging academic enthusiasm? Instead, homework is portrayed as a chore, and parents are portrayed as inept at helping. Adults buy into this stereotype, and therefore, parental conversations form children that expect education to be about checking off credits instead of emphasizing their joy at fulfilling their biblical role of being a lifetime mentor to their children.

The Bible teaches us to "Study to show yourself approved unto God" (2 Timothy 2:15), not approved unto an accreditation system. Now I'm all for the excellence that can be associated with accreditation, but it should be a partial measure, not the whole measure of successful educational. Until modern times, the church embraced an encyclopedia of information delivered through catechesis. The focus was on the unity of studying God's world and not the professional fragmentation and compartmentalization of subjects that mark the goal of modern education.

An Encyclopedia of Knowledge

The word "encyclopedia" has a very broad meaning.

"It contains three Greek components: en-cyclopedia. Padeia means teaching, and thus, 'encyclopedia' a complete circle or circuit of teaching. 'Theological encyclopedia' indicates the complete

circle or circuit of theological knowing, organized not alphabetically [emphasis mine], *but in terms of interrelationships of the several subject areas of knowledge.*" Muller, p.24 [2]

To the pre-modern church, encyclopedia did not refer to a body of knowledge designed around an alphabet. (Alphabetized encyclopedias are a great tool. I'm just pointing out the difference.) Instead it meant a systematic study of His Story, where you began with Genesis, went through the Bible, and then circled back to the beginning of the same stories. Each time a student studied the stories, they were expected to understand more of the Bible's meaning as he had a more mature brain and because the New Testament stories added definition to the earlier stories. Students were discipled to repeat often, or "re-sound" the Scriptures, the stories, the heroes' names, the creeds.

Then a dialectic conversation could occur between child and parent. "Are these stories familiar? Let's look again… Do you remember this hero being mentioned in a different Bible story? How do the two stories relate to each other? To the creed? To your life? Let's look again… Can you repeat to me the places, times, and situations where we meet Abraham? Can you explain how Abraham relates to Christ? Let's look again… Do you see Him? Is He in every Bible story?"

A parent disciples his or her children in the art of Bible study through discussions, like the one above, that bring the student back to the same point or information in many ways and guides the student to think about and connect ideas. We may begin with a didactic, or lecturing, style in order to transmit information (grammar), but we need to move into a Socratic, or dialectic, style in order to engage the student's brain.

The content taught through Christian discipleship until modern times included studying everything in creation, beginning with simple Bible stories and progressing through a cycle of learning language, math, science, music, economics, and more as the student came to understand their relationships to His Story. Keep in mind that science and math were often more applicable to pre-modern daily life than we technical moderns realize. It was easy for parents to teach math and science as a part of life. Understanding crop cycles, animal breeding, kitchen chemistry, and family economics divided those who ate well in the winter from those who starved. Notice all the farming and business parables Jesus used. Biblical idioms like "threshing floor" and "the skin of your teeth" meant more to Hebrew children than they do to us. Biblical laws protecting women and animals and slaves were far more humane than the Assyrian, or Roman, or Babylonian laws the biblical audience lived under, but they can sound oppressive to Americans. Our modern children are so sheltered from real life compared to a Hebrew child under Babylonian rule who had to farm to eat, hide to pray, or look forward to slavery to earn a living. Parents lived with their children around full-time until recently. They had plenty of opportunities to teach their children about everything as they walked, and talked, and sat down (Deuteronomy 6:7).

The encyclopedia of creation and Scripture and our conscience was only the content taught; the idea of catechesis was the goal. Whereas a modern encyclopedia is a good tool to own, the term needs to be recovered as educational content that teaches grammar, logic, and wisdom, while recapturing the true idea of an inter-connected universe with purpose.

Catechesis: Echo in Celebration

Moderns are taught that we live in a disconnected multi-verse without purpose. Catechesis— which means resounding or echoing in celebration — is the process by which persons were historically initiated into the Christian community and its faith, revelation, and vocation. I was born in the 1960's, yet I can remember going to Catechism School as a child. My own elder boys memorized a short catechism before becoming church members in the 1990's. Catechism as a method of passing on wisdom means more than memorizing an important list of doctrinal questions and answers, though it usually begins with memorizing creeds, laws, hymns, and prayers. Catechesis

> *"is the process by which persons throughout their lifetimes are continually converted and nurtured, transformed and formed, by and in (the church's) living tradition. [...] Every activity used by the church to celebrate and imitate the words or actions of God."* Westerhoff & Edwards, pp. 2-3.[3]

Catechism comes from the Greek meaning to resound or echo, to celebrate or initiate, to repeat another's words and deeds. This broad definition is useful in many other educational contexts. All of the educational models throughout history until the Enlightenment emphasized the idea of catechesis. It began with memorizing a set of facts and having the student echo the facts to a teacher. Then a discussion could begin that celebrated that information as God-given, and then used to initiate a student into a new world of thought. Knowledge wasn't designed to be left on the mind's grocery shelf. Instead, students need to pay attention to the many ways the rest of the ingredients at our disposal can be combined with new knowledge, so we may delight in preparing a nutritious recipe that adds the savor of Christ to our community. Holy laughter results from feasting on words and ideas with friends!

This model can be used to teach anyone anything with an expectant sense of joy when the knowledge is made personal, but more importantly when the information brings forth doxology, the desire to praise God for the order He has created. Biblical faith supports and enriches intellectualism. It rejects fragmentation that stops at specialization. Instead it rejoices in the unity of the whole person as they find God everywhere in creation.

In the 4th century, Augustine asked himself in his Soliloquies "What do you want to know?" He replied, "God and soul, nothing else!" He applied this idea to all of education — science, math, language, philosophy, and history.

> "So a doxological refrain pervades Augustine's Confessions; every good he experiences and all the truth he learns come ultimately from God and are occasions for praise." Westerhoff & Edwards, p. 26 [3]

Biblical faith supports and enriches intellectualism. It rejects fragmentation that stops at specialization. Instead it rejoices in the unity of the whole person as they find God everywhere in creation.

Some of the Old Testament books are difficult to enjoy, but after decades of Bible study, I know more about the sacrifices and symbols and how Jesus is manifested in the Old Testament ceremonies. Because my walk with the Lord has been longer now, I am a better Bible teacher to my younger sons than I ever was to the older. I wasn't very good at teaching the laws to Robert and John because I was just memorizing them myself.

I want to know as much as I can about the Bible, therefore I have read it many times. And I have read many other books that teach about the Bible. So, I now know more about other biblical cultures, butchering techniques, and Old Testament economics then when I first became a Christian. I have a better, though very incomplete, understanding of how the stories fore-shadow Christ, the church, and my place in it. I also have another ten years of seemingly unrelated life experiences to bear on His message. This encyclopedia of knowledge, gathered a little at a time over many years of study make the facts, the history, the Scriptures more delightful to me. They give me the ability to delight in the law of the Lord.

Many of you can say the same thing about a subject that you have spent years studying. I would be lying to my children if I told them they could say they had studied chemistry or Greek or temple sacrifices after reading one book with one teacher for one semester. They have only begun to study the grammar of that subject. Building a useful encyclopedia of knowledge that can be used wisely takes a long time.

Recently, we were reading about the Burnt Offering, the Grain Offering, and the Peace Offering. My boys found it funny that the Lord said the exact same paragraph over and over with just one word substituted like "bull" instead of "goat". We stopped and laughed a lot over words like "entrails" and wondered how people felt about dragging a dead beast to church. We also wondered if people resented giving the animals to God when they knew a poor person down the street could have used the food. Then we compared that thought to modern Christians who resent the cost of beautiful cathedrals, and how shallow an image of God they must have. Jesus said to give Him our best and that the poor would be with us always. Building cathedrals gives laborers honest jobs and rewards craftsmanship and hard work. I'm sure the poor would rather have a good job than a good handout. Building luxurious buildings are a testimony to God's provision to man. His provision is great so we should have enough resources to feed the poor and build cathedrals to honor Him. So, a verse describing the poor bringing a dove to the temple led to a discussion on modern economics and utilitarian attitudes among modern Christians.

Later, I spent time alone just giggling with the Lord because of the joy of having such wonderful conversations with my young boys. I asked Him why He said the same thing over and over. Why he didn't just use a chart? It would have been so much clearer and more efficient instead of paragraphs. I know if I'd have been a priest at the temple I would have hung out a large poster that listed the feasts, the specified offering size and parts for the first fruits, the portion to be left with the priest, the symbolic meaning of the blood, incense, and washings, etc. Then when someone wanted to know what to do with their pigeon I would have said, "Look at the chart." Kind of like the charts over the cashiers' heads at McDonald's. So I giggled at the thought of temple priests standing behind cash registers waiting for the temple visitors to decide on their choice of offering. Hmm… Maybe this is what helped make Jesus so angry when he pulled up to the drive-thru window at the temple and flipped over the money tables.

> *Learning makes you laugh, it makes you cry, and it can make you fall to your knees in humble repentance.*

I want to teach my children to set catechesis as their goal. I want to teach them to take an encyclopedic approach to learning by gathering up nuggets of facts, while weaving them through the grand themes of life, and developing a heart that sees God's blessings and provision everywhere. Learning makes you laugh, it makes you cry, and it can make you fall to your knees in humble repentance. Resounding Scripture, seeing it in larger and newer contexts, and teaching it to someone else allows us to echo His joy. Catechesis!

Echo In Celebration

A Universe with Purpose

Civil War Pastor Robert Dabney said a truly Christian education recognizes "Light as center", and that we live in a universe, not a multi-verse. American naturalist, John Muir, felt deeply connected to the created world. He said, "When

Catechesis: To Echo in Celebration

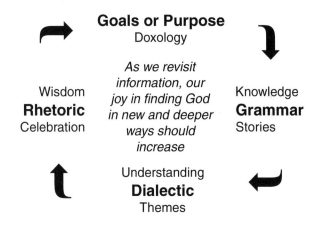

we try to pick out anything by itself we find it hitched to everything else in the universe." (*Exuberance: The Passion for Life*, p.32)[4] Just as the planets can be studied individually, they can be more successfully understood if studied in relationship to the sun. And each planet can be more completely understood if the other planets' characteristics and gravitational effects are included. The world was designed in an orderly manner that allows us to discover more and more reasons for doxology, praising our Creator.

Wilson "Snowflake" Bentley studied physics, meteorology, photography, chemistry, and word crafting all for the sake of preserving pictures of snowflakes. He tirelessly worked to capture for all mankind an unparallel collection of photographs of white crystals that continue to inspire us today. He actually would cry in remembrance of certain crystals that struck him as particularly beautiful. When he died, his hometown newspaper wrote,

> *"Wilson Bentley was a living example of this type of genius. He saw something in snowflakes which other men failed to see, not because they could not see, but because they had not the patience and understanding to look."*
> Burlington Free Press, Dec 28, 1931

Similarly, all academic subjects work together to bring glory to God, but our students often don't have the patience and understanding to look. So how do we give our children the gift of constant wonder at the created world and the Creator's words? How do we inspire them to be curious, to study in a manner that glorifies Him?

Learning should be illuminated by the light God gives us. The student needs to know that God has a plan for his or her life, but discovering that plan is a lifelong pursuit. For instance, I see in big pictures with specific goals. The future is as real to me as the present, but I'm lousy at the details. So I'll plow through just enough details to succeed in my vision. I like good grades so I worked hard at math in school. I like to travel so I worked hard in sales as a teen so I could win trips. I want to help children love God's word, so I study grammar. I want my boys to be great fathers, so I teach them to clean house and buy groceries. I wanted to fly rockets, so I studied aerospace engineering. I have done so much because I love to learn, not because I'm any good at the things I listed. I like the results more than the process. So, I don't want to be labeled as a math person or a language person or an artsy type. I'm willing to do any work if it gets me to my goal. In the process, I discovered that one of my gift's is the ability to see the basics of a subject and show others what I see so they can also learn how to learn. Pursuing the passions that He gave me led me to His purpose for my life.

Moderns praise God when inspired by a sunset, a baby's birth, or a full harvest from a persistent endeavor, but we forget to be grateful to be allowed to just breathe. We are excited by new ideas, new technologies, and new adventures, but we forget to honor the past, relish the mundane, and bless the common things in life. If all that we see, from stars in the distance to DNA under a microscope, declare God's amazing bounty and His creation's beauty, then a broad base of learning should teach us to honor God by hungering to know more about His mysteries — the simple and the exciting. Worship can be centered in study that is integrated and inclusive. Academic subjects are just the categories of creation, the aisles and shelves. Making a great recipe takes understanding and wisdom!

Utilitarianism, teaching only what is useful, is a poor educational model for free men. True education is more than useful or pragmatic. It

> *... all academic subjects work together to bring glory to God, but our students often don't have the patience and understanding to look.*

is beautiful and inspiring. I want to be useful and I want to work hard, because it gives Him joy to say 'Well done, my faithful servant." I want my children to be prepared to love living wisely for the Lord anywhere and in any situation in which He sends them. Knowledge advances primarily through the work of specialists, but for the specialist to be most effective, he must understand the integrative context in which he works. So we should not react against specialization, per se, but rather against disconnected, non-unified/ integrative specialization.

For example, I am so happy we have brain surgeons. The advancement in their specialization provides joy and hope and peace for many people. But all that advancement is for nothing if we can't sift it through the filter of economics, psychology, and ethics. Humans are not machines. So I am glad for the advancements in university departments of economics, psychology, and ethics, too. If I needed a brain surgeon, I would have to sort out very many ideas besides the quality of my surgeon's skills. I would have to evaluate my family's needs, my own desires, the Lord's will, and the cost to everyone involved. I would have to know how to think in the midst of great stress. I would be grateful that as an educated person I know how to get a bank loan to pay for bills, fill out insurance forms to help cover some expenses, be able to pray with my family, be able to weigh the information from multiple surgeons' opinions, and so on. Do I need to study brain surgery to have brain surgery? No. But I have a long history of miscarried babies, and I know how stressful and emotional medical decisions can be. Every time I have had to make a medical decision, I am always grateful I know how to learn.

True education should prepare us to love learning and to see the world from God's side of the sky. Learning should affect the heart as much as the head. We should help our students look for challenging mentors more than easy text books. The original role of education in the church was to have students discipled by someone who looked out for their whole heart — a lover of Christ who transferred his or her delight in the Lord, someone to show students that they could receive His blessings now. As C.S. Lewis put it, "Pleasures are shafts of God's glory touching our sensibilities." Christians must feast each Sunday, rest in His peace, sing out His praises, and seek Him everywhere. We are called to joy in spite of life's difficulties.

My eight-year-old son, David, is currently delighted that he has two rows of bottom teeth like a shark. We went to the dentist to see about this wonderful problem. When I told the dentist about David's shark's teeth the dentist began to tell us about the amazing diversity of sharks' teeth. When he was finished telling David his story, I commented, "I'm sure every one of those teeth was perfectly designed by someone who knew just what He was doing." I look for Him everywhere so I can teach my children to delight in Him. Fortunately the dentist concurred about our incredible Creator, but more importantly, David heard every word. I want him to know that we can learn from the dentist and share God's love at the same time.

> *True education should prepare us to love learning and to see the world from God's side of the sky.*

I want our family to know the joy of catechesis. We learn shark facts because they enable us to share the gospel; we learn grammar because we want to write praise songs; we study math because we want to be good stewards of resources and talents. So we read the same stories over and over. We write the same verb conjugations over and over. We write out every step of a math problem. We practice sitting still. We practice drawing. We sing favorite songs until we know the words by heart. We say the same Bible verse again and again. We discuss the themes and principles of the information we learn and how the information can help us to live wisely. We re-sound until one day a new idea blooms in our brain and we grasp its importance so quickly and so profoundly and with such delight that we can't help but laugh! We celebrate our life's purpose — to know God and to make Him known!

[1] Reed, Jeff 1996. *The 7th Priority* LearnCorp.

[2] Muller, Richard A. 1991. *The Study of Theology: From Biblical Interpretation to Contemporary Formulation.* Grand Rapids, MI: Zondervan.

[3] Westerhoff III, John H. & Edwards Jr., O.C. 1981. *A Faithful Church: Issues in the History of Catechesis.* Morehouse Publishing Company.

[4] Dabney, Robert, *Securalized Education* Retrieved Aug. 2006 from the World Wide Web: http://wellingtonchristianschools.org.nz/dabney.pdf

Chapter Eight

The Priority: Preparing for Opportunities

> "Nay, the same Solomon the king, although he excelled in the glory of treasure and magnificent buildings, of shipping and navigation, of service and attendance, of fame and renown, and the like, yet he maketh no claim to any of these glories, but only to the glory of inquisition of truth; for so he saith expressly, "The glory of God is to conceal a thing, but the glory of the king is to find it out"; as if, according to the innocent play of children, the Divine Majesty took delight to hide his works, to the end to have them found out; and as if kings could not obtain a greater honour than to be God's play-fellows in that game."
> —Francis Bacon, *The Advancement of Learning*, 1605

This morning, our family woke up and read two chapters from the Bible while we snuggled in bed. We discussed what the Old Testament passages meant in reference to the New Testament and how we live our lives. We reviewed our memory work from John 1:1-12 and prayed for the brothers at college. Then we showered, ate, and straightened up the house. Afterwards, we all sat at our dining room table. William and David worked on math while my husband, Rob, and I discussed previous Federal Reserve chairmen Paul Volker and Alan Greenspan now that Mr. Bernanke has been appointed to take over. William was interested in our conversation so we stopped to explain who the most powerful man in the world really is and how much better economic times are for our family now than 20 years ago. Rob calculated some statistics from *USA Today* in reference to these men, and we talked in admiration of a job well done. We are often able to include Rob in these teachable moments because we chose to live a life centered around our home rather than offices or school buildings. As technology opens up work options, we believe more families will want to explore a similar lifestyle.

Rob was able to retire in his 40's even though it was very hard to save money in the early years of our marriage. He always had a vision and a goal. Plus he is exceptionally disciplined and taught himself how to invest money well by reading financial magazines. I recently made a new acquaintance who was intrigued that Rob was willing to retire early. She said her husband, an oil executive, always wondered when the savings would really be enough and that kept him working. (For an intriguing look at wealth in America, read Thomas J. Stanley's *The Millionaire Next Door.*[1])

Her comment and others like it got me thinking about why we just aren't concerned about money like others apparently are. Maybe we are very foolish to have retired early. Our eldest son, Robert says we need to explain ourselves better to the relatives since they are worried about our finances. My husband delights in keeping them guessing and just chuckles when they voice concern. He never gives them a straight answer. But the real answer isn't in our financial investments or in the bank. It's in the value of our talents. We like to work; we like to study; we like to try new things. No financial advisors would ever be comfortable suggesting early retirement based on our financial wealth. In fact, these should be our highest earning years, as Rob was at the top of his career. Financial advisors measure wealth with modern standards just like schools measure success with modern standards. Well, they aren't our standards.

Rethinking the Priorities

The classical model of education, especially for our family as Christians, measures wealth in relationships and talents. We pursue love, life, and learning in that order. When Robert was born and I went to work, Rob refused to put Robert in daycare. He stayed home with Robert until I decided to stay home. Then he worked hard at jobs where he could go into work very early and have long evenings with us at home. When William and David were born, we made lifestyle changes so both Rob and I could be home with them. He missed too much of Robert and John's childhood. William and David are already getting to the point where Mom and Dad aren't needed 24/7 so we're beginning to work longer hours away from home. One of us is always home with them, and very often the four of us are together. We've already launched two children and know how short our time is with William and David. Plus, people live a lot longer these days. We have plenty of years to work 60 hour weeks once our "little boys" are grown and we're well insured should something happen to prevent that possibility.

> *The classical model of education, especially for our family as Christians, measures wealth in relationships and talents.*

The point is we work to live, not that we live to work. Now if you know us at all that doesn't mean we're lazy. Robert and John will tell you that I don't know the meaning of not working. I just want to work surrounded by loved ones, and technology has made that possible. I want our work to serve as a form of discipleship for these boys we're raising. I expect them to be productive adults who give a lot of time to their families, so we need to model that for them. Americans talk about the rat race but rarely leave it. We never even joined it.

The confidence we have that we'll be financially secure comes from the Lord and honoring that He wants us to put our family first. For some reason the Lord has given us a deep, deep hunger to learn how to use the talents he gave us. When people worry about money and jobs, what they are really saying is, "I don't know how to develop all the gifts and talents God gave me, so I need to depend on others to provide employment for me." We prefer to look for the next opportunity. Sometimes it may be a job. Other times it may be self-employment. As we get older, it is more often an investment. We don't feel that our college degrees or employment choices define us. They just added to our opportunities. We both continue to invest in classes and in self-education.

> We can always make more money. We can't make more time.

The classical model and a Home-Centered Education foster a love for life and learning. The fear of the Lord is the beginning of wisdom, and knowing He is our provision makes it easy to put our children ahead of money. The irony is that every time we've made a conscious choice as a couple to pursue family life over career, we've had an enormous growth in our income. It used to make Robert and John crazy because as soon as we had some extra money, we'd quit working at that task and begin a new adventure. We can always make more money. We can't make any more time.

Prepare for Opportunities

When you know how to learn, you can do anything, and you can try new things without fear. And when opportunities to use your talents present themselves, you will already be prepared to take steps forward. It's exciting to see our grown boys look for similar opportunities.

I had the pleasure of staying at a very expensive home. The kind movie stars rent to get away from it all. I made the erroneous initial conclusion that the family that owned the home was very rich. I was wrong. Turned out they were very smart and had paid very little for their amazing facility. The family had lived in the region a long time and had recently taken the knowledge they had of the local economy and basically made some wise bartering decisions to get the land. Then they used the resources on the land to build the home themselves with some sub-contracting. We're talking multi-millions in value for thousands in costs. I found some definite kindred spirits who loved sharing their story with me. I learned a lot about the timber and land development industry and now know more questions to ask the next time I am interested in real estate.

Every adult who is naturally good at something uses very specific tools in learning more about their field and perfecting the art of doing what they love. Sit back and be self-evaluative about how you learn the things you love and then apply the same techniques to things that are new or hard. I love the *Rich Dad, Poor Dad* books by Robert T. Kiyosaki because they help to change the thoughts people have about education and money. Our thought life controls us and sets us up either for failure or success. My favorite new thought from *Rich Dad, Poor Dad* is when the author learned to stop saying, "I don't have the money for that" and replaced it with this new thought — "How can I get the money for that?"[2] The first (and more common) response shuts down possibilities. It is negative. The second thought allows access to the entire world of possibilities. It launches another adventure.

Fear of new jobs, careers, and situations is what keeps people from reaching their potential. I want our boys to be

> *When you know how to learn, you can do anything.*

able to do all things through Christ who strengthens them. I want them to fear Him, not the world. Our boys may one day be engineers building a bridge in a foreign land. We want them to know how to learn any language well so they can learn the native tongue quickly and become managers and negotiators of projects sooner than if they had to struggle with the language. Or they may be linguists on a mission to a foreign land and have to set up a budget and accounting system for the enterprise funding them. Or maybe they'll be rock stars who need to be money smart so they don't end up in bankruptcy hearings. We just want them prepared for anything. We want them truly educated in the sense of a liberal education, where liberal is the Latin root for "free." To study to be free requires you to work very hard at practicing the tools of freedom.

In *Angels in the Architecture*, author Douglas Wilson points out that even the poorest married couple in the world can delight in one another and glorify God through their marriage union[3]. I propose that the same thing is true about our minds. It costs nothing to think; your brain is always conveniently with you; and there is a feast of ideas to savor. Wasn't it Augustine who said, "Civilization consists of conversation"? If you want to have interesting conversations with your children and similar confidence in facing life, then you must practice, practice, practice learning!

Enter the Great Classical Conversations

Beowulf, C.S. Lewis, Roman architecture, music and art, American History, Macbeth, sports heroes, Julius Caesar, Plato, Freud. How do you enter into the Great Classical Conversations these words invoke? You have to read, take classes, read, discuss, read, read, and read. It's work. While a love for book learning doesn't ensure living well, it does enable one to learn from the mistakes of people that you will never meet. Reading enables the reader to hear ideas foreign to his or her surroundings without having to travel. Reading takes the collective wealth of mankind's knowledge and puts it at the reader's fingertips. Non-readers can only learn from local experiences. Readers can learn from others' experiences.

You could argue that listening to someone on a CD or TV show offers the same opportunity, but I would disagree. It is much easier to contemplatively evaluate an idea word by word when it is written down on a page you are holding than if you have to go back and forth by pushing a button on a machine. Active readers often lay their books down on their lap to think about an idea, and then they reread the same words again and again. This is easier to do with a book. You can write on the page, dog-leaf the corner, and even cuddle with the volume in a warm bed. Books encourage evaluation rather than indoctrination.

Anyone with an average IQ or higher can read well with practice, so if you aren't a great reader, start with children's books like the Newbery winners. I had to read these "easier" books before I could read modern classics. Then, after that I was able to enjoy reading modern classics, I could move onto the more difficult ancient classics. Intensive Bible studies also improved my reading ability, as did a quick course in phonics and spelling rules.

Preparing yourself will give you more opportunities to learn the skills needed to participate in the Great Classical Conversations with your children. Conversations can open up new ideas, perspectives, and experiences that will enlarge your family's outlook on the temporal, the eternal, the nature of man, the streams of history, the purpose of leadership and service, the price of freedom, and our personal responsibilities. You student's situation, purpose in life, and personality will dictate how he or she serves the Lord. Your job is to equip them with the tools of learning and that includes three things — how to study words well (grammar), how to process thoughts logically (dialectic), and how to wisely act upon the logic of those thoughts (rhetoric).

Conversations can open up new ideas, perspectives, and experiences...

I spend each day in awe of our blessings and pray that I can help more families love Home-Centered Education. It offers so much more than just a good practical education. Parents can find teachers, both living and in books, that light fires for the whole family. I know it can foster a family's desire to enter the Great Classical Conversations of history, faith, philosophy, and science. Home-Centered Education can give families the freedom to live in a way that honors God's priorities while providing an opportunity to explore possibilities we never imagined. The only reasonable response? Celebration! Celebrate and listen to it echo throughout your house!

[1] Stanley, Thomas J. & Danko, William D. 1998. *The Millionaire Next Door.* Longstreet Press.

[2] Kiyosaki, Robert & Lechter, Sharon 2000. *Rich Dad, Poor Dad.* Warner Books Ed.

[3] Jones, Douglas & Wilson, Douglas 1998. *Angels in the Architecture: A Protestant Vision for Middle Earth.* Canon Press.

Chapter Nine

The Offering: Discipling the Human Heart

> *"Julia (Butterfly) Hill sat in a tree she named 'Luna' for 2 years to save it from being chopped down."*
> —*Forbes 2006 Investment Issue,* Dec. 12, 2005

This book was hard to write for two reasons. First, I struggle to write well. And second, I don't want anyone to think they should emulate our family, as I know we all need to find solutions that work for our own unique situations. So by sharing the stories of our family and friends' families, it feels like I'm bragging. In all honesty, I guess I am sometimes. But my intention is to challenge you to think about new opportunities in Home-Centered Education that may help your family embrace the love of life and learning. Only real people are invited to participate.

Our family is not perfect and we do fall apart. I could share some of my children's sinful natures but that is their story to reveal and not mine. Let's just say as parents we have had to deal with "sex, drugs, and rock'n'roll" more often than we care to. We never sheltered our older boys. We actually gave them unusual amounts of freedom. And because they are sinners, they have made foolish decisions. William and David are entering the age where we will give them more freedom in the context of pursuing the passions God has formed in their hearts. That means we will have to deal with their foolishness. Whenever I pick up a son from a friend's house, I always ask, "Did he behave himself?" I fully expect the answer to be "No", and I fully expect my children to know they will be held accountable when the answer is "No". I do this for two reasons. To assure other adults that mentor them that I respect their judgment and want to be told the truth about their behavior and to remind my children that I am always expecting them to live up to the responsibility of being ambassadors for Christ. The name "Bortins" is very powerful, in that we want it to remind the people we encounter of the goodness of God. We are His earthly representatives. He calls us His ambassadors. We are His heirs and therefore, we are royalty. It's hard to live up to the responsibility of being servant-leaders without His power and grace!

Mr. Keller or Annie Sullivan?

We all know the story of *The Miracle Worker*. Poor Helen Keller was deaf, mute, and blind due to an illness in infancy. Her parents loved her so much that they let her always have her way because life was just so hard and so unfair to their beloved daughter. As is true any time a child gets her way all the time, they were raising a beast instead of a human. Life was ugly and feelings were hurt. But they knew in their hearts that something should be done to help her cope, and so, Mr. and Mrs. Keller applied for a teacher to come live with them. Annie Sullivan joined their lives. The real miracle isn't what Annie Sullivan did; it's that they found someone like Annie Sullivan at all.

The parents looked at dear Helen and prayed for a child that wouldn't embarrass them. They prayed for a child who could just behave. To be able to speak with her seemed an impossible dream. Annie looked at Helen and saw a child who could be independent and self-sufficient. She was so frustrated with the Keller's low expectations. The Kellers looked at Helen and saw learning disabilities and limitations. They saw what Helen liked and didn't like. Annie looked at Helen and saw a woman who would one day speak to kings and write for nations.

Which kind of parent or educator are you? A Mr. Keller or an Annie Sullivan? We all have a world view, a foundational way of thinking. Is yours that we are what we are and should act according to our nature? I am a Christian woman who believes we are to rise above our natures and equip our children to do the same. We are to look at our children and say, "Child, you are called to lead great causes for Christ and I want you equipped to show the world the fruit of the Spirit."

My friend, Jeanine, is one of my many heroines. Her eldest of four children was born blind. Jeanine and her husband have a hope in their heart for their daughter and a trust in the Lord that He will only bless them and not curse them. So it was not odd to them to have three more children. Raising a blind child requires patience and hard work. I'm sure it is hard on their whole family at times, especially since Jeanine and her husband choose to focus on Home-Centered Education.

> *Which kind of parent or educator are you? A Mr. Keller or an Annie Sullivan?*

Jeanine wants the best for all of her children and she knows no one will investigate options and make choices with the love and thoroughness she puts into it. So she brings some instructors into her home, goes out with her children to others, and teaches them certain things herself. Because her daughter is blind, Jeanine learned to use technology to her advantage long before most parents even thought of it. The easiest thing for her as a busy mother of three other children would be to put her daughter in a full time educational institution. At least that's what experts advised. But their pursuit of love, life and learning revolves around the family. So instead of taking an easier route, her family pays a lot of money to have textbooks translated into Braille. There are wonderful books translated into Braille already, but they aren't always the books Jeanine wants to use. When they are finished with the text, they donate the texts to blind services in case someone else wants to travel a similar path. These parents know the cost of ignorance is far higher than the $600 they pay per translated algebra book.

What about their other children? They become annoyed by their sister like any other kids. They also see their sister model daily the meaning of hard work. They must keep the house picked up and items put away or they would make life hard for their sister. What excellent training they receive in doing things for others! One day it was this family's turn to do a performance for their Classical Conversations' program. As you can imagine, they performed a piece of music since that is something all four children can do together. It was a nice presentation with polite applause, but there wasn't a dry eye in the audience when a younger brother rushed to his blind sister's elbow to guide her down the stage's unfamiliar stairs. Thank you, Jeanine, for choosing to honor God through your family's example. You are an Annie Sullivan.

I have another friend who was in a serious car accident and literally has half of her brain damaged. She is a fine woman who works part time as a nurse while using her home as the center of her children's education. When she enrolled her daughter in Classical Conversations in the 7th grade, she had done very little academic instruction beyond teaching her daughter to read. Kitty, the mother, had good intentions but was obviously handicapped by her own abilities to retain information, as her short-term memory is damaged. A modern school teacher would probably believe the family was neglectful. But this family knew there is more to educating an entire human than training the mind. She also wanted to protect her children's hearts and disciple them into a love for Christ. That is very hard to do when they are gone from you the better part of their childhood.

Well, the other tutors and I encouraged this student, and chuckled at some of her attempts to do assignments, but loved her kind heart and her continuing efforts. Neither she nor her mother gave up; they both took additional courses trying to understand the classical model. And we always saw improvement. Anna, who loved her parents, worked hard at difficult assignments and became our very best student the year she turned 16. Her character was trained to please her parents and obey her tutors; therefore, her academic skills were able to make great leaps when she reached an adult level of maturity and abstract reasoning. Thank you, Kitty. You are an Annie Sullivan.

We had another high school student who was born with a totally unfair proportion of beauty and social skills. Her parents desired more for her academic life than she desired for herself in high school and enrolled her in our academically challenging tutorial program. Her tutors saw a common mix of great academic potential distracted by a youthful desire to maximize her natural assets. Her mother talked to myself and her other tutors about this distraction and was willing to listen to any suggestions we had. Once you get into the higher levels of our tutorials, the students are constantly writing papers and making presentations on

"Why" things happen and are challenged to enter the Great Classical Conversations of the past. About mid-year of this young woman's junior year, I saw the change begin. Her school work improved immensely. She became a leader in the class. She corrected my errors. And then one day it happened. To me, it's like magic. She told me at lunch one day, "I'm not dating anyone until I get out of college. It's such a distraction from school and the things I want to do." She kept her promise through the rest of high school and had an incredible senior year. When I was helping her think through college applications, she said to me the words I like to hear out of every senior, "I don't know what I want to major in. I like studying everything." Her parents fought with her (and for her) rather than allowing their daughter to settle in her vanity, and temporal, short-sighted desires. It is hard to be an Annie Sullivan.

> *Her parents fought with her (and for her) rather than allowing their daughter to settle in her vanity, and temporal, short-sighted desires*

Sacrifices and Offerings

A few years ago, my teens and I went to a lecture on education and economics from a very poor woman from Africa. She told us her family only made $1500 a year and yet spent $1000 a year on their children's educations. She was in her twenties and knew without a shadow of a doubt the most important thing to her parents — her and her siblings being given opportunities to love life and learning. No wonder she loved speaking on education to economists around the world. The District of Columbia spends over $13,000 a year per student. So obviously, money doesn't make a good education. She told us she succeeded because her parents constantly sacrificed to provide for and direct her education. What percentage of income do Americans spend on educating their children? In America, a parent who chooses to stay home full-time with their children sacrifices more than $30,000 a year plus benefits and career advancement. Obviously, our children will recognize what we truly value. No matter how loud teens scream that they want their independence, they want someone to love and respect even more. When we reflect on high school, it was the "hard" teachers we remember with respect. Adults that teach children to rise above their natural gifts and learn to do hard things eventually are appreciated.

Another former student was working at a grocery store and was considered odd because she home schooled and didn't date. She's very beautiful and the other employees knew she didn't date because she turned down all the many requests. Another checkout girl asked Carrie about a ring on her finger. Carrie explained that it was from her father to remind her that his job was to love and protect her until God brought the right man into her life to take over that task. Instead of thinking that was silly, the check out girl responded that she wished her father would just think about her, let alone promise to protect her.

Do you love your children as much as Julia (Butterfly) Hill loved her tree? Are you willing to pay a lot of money for texts books like Jeannine? Are you willing to trust God like Kitty? Are you ready to see your daughters as princesses who deserve the security of knowing

> *The sacrifices you offer, while intentionally discipling your children, are a fragrant aroma to the Lord.*

they are loved by their father? Are you ready to hold your children to a godly standard when they are flirting with this world? Are you willing to sacrifice the majority of your income for your children's education?

The sacrifices you offer, while intentionally discipling your children, are a fragrant aroma to the Lord. My friend, Janet says to her children, "It's OK for you to hate me for a season so you will love me for a lifetime." Jim Elliot said it best. "He is no fool who gives what he can not keep to gain that which he can not lose." We humbly submit the offering, and He changes the human heart.

Chapter Ten

The Call:
Living and Learning
In Celebration

"The end then of learning is to repair the ruins of our first parents by regaining to know God aright, and out of that knowledge to love him, to imitate him, to be like him, as we may the nearest by possessing our souls of true virtue, which being united to the heavenly grace of faith makes up the highest perfection".

—John Milton, *Of Education,* 1644

This book is merely "the call" to a Home-Centered Education. The details I have left to other books. I have given you just a taste of the tools of learning, the academic abilities of our country when everyone knew the tools of learning, and a few stories about modern families that are successfully recovering the tools of learning.

I began with a little information on the problem with modern education, how technology is reshaping our culture, and the desire of home schooling pioneers to help other parents think about the possibilities of new educational models. Entering into new paradigms usually takes some kind of startling revelation; otherwise, it is too hard to break the habits of a lifetime.

I remember when I first began helping parents teach math to their children, they initially labeled me as a math person, and I let them. One day a mom found out how much I loved analyzing literature in relationship to history and economics and said to me, "Hmm… I thought you were a math person." I had defined myself in terms of my college degree. I went home with a new buzz in my brain. I had defined myself as a math person, because I was raised in a school system that placed a limiting label on me. From that moment on, I realized I just liked to learn about a lot of things. Was I just odd? Weren't there all these left-brain right-brain studies and learning style studies and giftedness matrixes in educational circles? What boxes was I putting my children in by using confining definitions and assumptions? So I developed a new thought to tell myself. Instead of saying "This is hard, I'm no good at it," I switched to "This is hard, I wonder how I could make it easy?" In life, we are what we think. I found out I could think my way successfully into a wide range of adventures and opportunities.

Who knew that this aerospace engineer would one day be a writer on culture and education? Who knew that this girl trained to have a career would give birth to four boys? Who knew that women all over America would one day be astounded that I could remember their name and story after speaking with them one time a year or more ago? No

> *For many parents, the secret gift of Home-Centered Education is that we finally receive the education we never had.*

teacher ever would have predicted my future accurately, including my parents. If I can retrain my brain, you can do it too! I am amazed at the new brain power I've received after a relatively short amount of time working hard at teaching my children to learn. Our family is recovering the lost tools of learning two generations at a time. For many parents, the secret gift of Home-Centered Education is that we finally receive the education we never had.

If I can direct the education of my children, you can do it, too. I don't have a teaching degree. I am quick to get angry. I am slow to listen. I don't eat right, and I am not a math person. I am just a sinner who falls short of the glory of God, but I know that I can do all things through Christ who strengthens me. The Bible addresses parents when it comes to commands about teaching our children. The problem for moderns is that we think that God's laws don't include math facts or parts of speech. Jesus calls himself the Word, so we should hunger to know everything about words. He tells us creation reveals His glory, so we should be delighted to learn math and science. He commands us to sing praise to Him, so we should work at learning musical notes. Everything is His, so we should learn the tools of learning everything. He doesn't try to trick us or make things too hard for us. Everything in creation is supported by a foundational structure. Everything in creation has an orderly design. Everything in creation glorifies Him. No one can ever know everything, but most of us can learn how to know anything if we use the designed order as our foundation.

The cry of every parent's heart is to see their child prosper and succeed; to succeed as students, family members, community members, and as citizens of heaven. Yet we, as parents, are not expected to teach our children. Temporary professionals, who move quickly in and out of our children's lives, are given this job. I wish as a child someone had

> *The cry of every parent's heart is to see their child prosper and succeed; to succeed as students, family members, community members, and as citizens of heaven.*

taken responsibility for my education and said, "Leigh, in 40 years you are going to have children with their own deep personal struggles and important talents to share with the world. You do not have the maturity to understand why learning to learn is important now, but you will be very grateful one day when you are helping your children make educational decisions. I will not just teach you about the things you like to do, because your children, spouse, boss, and neighbors may need you to do things you do not like to do. I will prepare you to learn any information and use it well."

So what if your child has ADHD, or is a kinesthetic learner, or just doesn't like reading? Are you going to see a deaf, dumb, and blind victim or are you going to see someone who can influence world leaders? Will you define your child by their weakness or by their potential? Do you believe your child can grow in grace and favor before God and men? Do you really believe your children are made in God's image? Or are they just another animal, a species of Planet Earth? Will they live forever? Or do we need to let them eat, drink, and be merry for tomorrow they will die?

It is very hard work to teach children "to love Him, to imitate Him, to be like Him" in a home-centered environment, but the Psalms say that the joy of the Lord is our strength. Since every reference in the Bible about teaching is given to parents or church leaders, it follows that Christians should provide the majority of a youth's instruction. To think otherwise is to trust non-Christians to teach your children the wisdom of God; to act as though knowledge is neutral. I want my children to know I value sharing Christ and His creation with them, and that there is no greater honor for me than being God's play-fellow with them. This may sound impossible to you, but if you seek first the kingdom of God, you will have those magic moments when your children know their home resides on holy ground.

America's current school model takes the role of prime educator away from parents. So parents don't know how to be a consistent adult watching out for their children's best academic interests. As soon as a first grader, especially a first grader from a bad family situation, gives trust and feels love to that all important first grade teacher, we rip their relationship apart and tell that child to start all over again with a new second grade teacher. We teach the student that the person, their teacher, isn't important; moving to the next grade is important. True education is centered around relationship and mentoring — discipleship.

School is changing... fast. Technology and globalism have made institutional education antiquated. We need to shift our thinking as to the best way to educate our children. We need to tell students that learning is hard and requires a lot of hours of work for the students, parents, and teachers. We need to be goal oriented in skills and look for the best disciplers of our children. We need to understand education begins and ends with relationship.

It's been ten years since I stumbled upon the teaching tools and philosophy used in American one-room school houses. I am not endorsing one-room school houses, but learning the teaching techniques used in that era has reshaped what Home-Centered Education looks like for our family. These teaching tools have made my job as an educator easier, and it has forced me to evaluate the future of our second pair of sons very differently than the first pair. I want to take the successful teaching skills of America's past and apply them to the technology of the future using the globe as our classroom. I want to recover not just the lost tools of learning, but encourage every parent to recover the joy of catechesis — learning that leads families to praise the Lord together.

JRR Tolkien masterfully described the cry of my heart when he had Bilbo write:

> *"I sit beside the fire and think of people long ago,*
> *And people who will see a world that I shall never know.*
> *But all the while I sit and think of times there were before,*
> *I listen for returning feet and voices at the door."*
> (From Bilbo's Song, Tolkien, p. 307)[1]

I pray that the greatest joy in your life will be the sound of your children's footsteps and voices at your door. My humble prayer is that in some way I have inspired you to open the door of your heart and allowed the echo of our family's celebration to enter. I pray that eventually the rooms in your home will be filled with the echo of your family's celebrations while learning all things unto His glory.

---

[1] Tolkien, J.R.R. 1999. *The Fellowship of the Ring.* Boston, MA: Houghton-Mifflin.

Statistical Resources

The Statistics quoted about modern education are from the National Assessment of Educational Progress (NAEP). NAEP research is paid for by American taxpayers and their data is available for all to see for free at http://nces.ed.gov/nationsreportcard/.

Other

Even though I didn't include the following resources in this book, please visit them for more information on the success of Home-Centered Education in its current form.

The National Home Education Research Institute has very interesting statistics that are available at http://www.nheri.org/ .

The Home School Legal Defense Association acts as a lobby group for home schools and has also collected some very interesting data at http://hslda.org/.

For information from NAEP on Homeschooled Children, go to http://nces.ed.gov/programs/coe/2005/pdf/03_2005.pdf

For the outcomes of 12th graders in 2005 go to http://nces.ed.gov/programs/coe/2007/section2/indicator11.asp where it says

> *"The percentage of 12th-graders performing at or above Basic decreased from 80 to 73 percent, and the percentage performing at or above Proficient*

decreased from 40 to 35 percent between 1992 and 2005."

That means only 35 percent of our graduating 12th graders in 2005 were proficient readers. The rest were basic or below.

The National Assessment of Educational Progress (NAEP) conducts long-term trend assessments, which provide information on changes in the basic achievement of America's youth since the early 1970s. They are administered nationally and report student performance at ages 9, 13, and 17 in reading and mathematics. Measuring trends of student achievement or change over time requires the precise replication of past procedures. Therefore, the long-term trend instrument does not evolve based on changes in curricula or in educational practices.

Home-Centered Education

www.ClassicalConversations.com offers a lot more information about curriculum, philosophy, calendar of free events like our Parent Practicums, locations of Classical Conversations Communities, and links to forums and classical web sites.

www.ClassicalConversationsBooks.com offers hundreds of books used by classical educators both in schools and at home. This is also where we take registration for our popular Student Academic Camps.

www.AcademicRecords.net is a very powerful record keeper that helps students at home or in private academies build a great transcript, report card, or resume to include with scholarship and college applications.

Our *Words Aptly Spoken* series will help students and adults new to life-long learning enter the Great Classical Conversations.

The *Foundations Guide* from Classical Conversations will lead parents through an excellent grammar program for children 4-12 years old.

Our *Challenge Program Directors* offer dialectic and rhetorical programs for students 12 -18 years old through weekly tutorials.

Our upcoming Echo in Celebration series:

The Foundations of Home-Centered Education

The Essentials of Home-Centered Education

The Challenge of Home-Centered Education